A Different Story

Trusting the Greatest Author with Your "Still Single" Chapter

LIANNA MUELLER, M.A.

Table of Contents

Acknowledgments.. i

Preface iii

Chapter 1: A Peaceful Heart............................. 1

Chapter 2: No Limits 11

Chapter 3: On Jealousy and the Journey............... 19

Chapter 4: Against Discouragement 25

Chapter 5: Let's Talk Genealogy 35

Chapter 6: Where is The Church? 43

Chapter 7: A Different Calling 51

Chapter 8: Divine Protection............................. 59

Chapter 9: Obedience and Trust 65

Chapter 10: Renouncing Fear 71

Chapter 11: A Time for Healing 77

Chapter 12: The Gifts of Wisdom & Clarity............ 89

Chapter 13: Openness.................................... 99

Chapter 14: A Suitable Partner 103

Chapter 15: The Chapter on Chastity 109

Chapter 16: The Gift of Time and Seasons........... 121

Chapter 17: A Loving Community 129

Chapter 18: Prayer 135

Chapter 19: Faithfulness.. 139

Chapter 20: Surrender 145

Chapter 21: Faith and Hope for the Future.......... 157

Epilogue.. 167

Recommended Reading.. 171

My Different Story 173

Acknowledgments

$\mathcal{F}$irst and foremost, I would like to dedicate this book to the Author of my story and life. You have walked with me through everything. You have had a plan for each chapter of my life and known how each chapter would build upon the next. I don't know what's up ahead, but I know that You are always faithful. I love You more than anything and anyone. All I want is to serve You and be everything that You intend for me to be. I'm excited about the further adventures that you have planned.

This book is also dedicated to anyone who has encouraged me on this journey and in my identity as a beloved daughter of God. A very special "thank you" goes out to Nicole Miller. Thank you for answering my abundance of questions about the book writing process and for looking over many of these chapters. You are such an inspiration to me. Your "different story" has given me greater courage to live mine. Another special "thank you" goes to my family for being so supportive and encouraging. As the years go on, I realize how blessed I am to have such a wonderful family! There are many others who have prayed for and encouraged me in this writing journey and the process of becoming who I'm meant to be. I don't want to leave anyone out, but you know who you are! There are too many of you to name. I love you all deeply, and words can't express my gratitude.

I would like to send a special acknowledgment out to all of you who know the pain of having a deep desire of your heart unfulfilled. This especially goes out to all those who are still single, never expecting that this would continue to be your path. I pray that you find hope and encouragement, and also realize that you are not alone, as you read this book.

A special dedication goes out to my mama in Heaven, Deborah Mueller. Thank you for giving me life. I know you intercede for me daily. For that, I am eternally grateful!

Preface

"No one told me!"** I lamented to Nicole one evening as we shared our hearts, discussing our unexpected life circumstances. "No one ever told me that I could be 28 and still single." She suggested that I write a blog post with that title. I didn't write a blog post. I began to write and didn't stop! Three years later, here's an entire book about this topic instead.

Perhaps it sounds silly that I assumed that I would have been married by 28. Sometimes, we build up unconscious expectations and hopes for our lives. Other times, these expectations and hopes have been built up for us by others, society, and even our own churches. These expectations become so deeply rooted in our lives that it becomes painful when they do not come to fruition. It's like buying a ticket to a much-awaited destination and then waiting, with the ticket in your hand, for a plane that never shows up. It could also be compared to getting on the plane and ending up somewhere drastically different than the place you planned on going!

During my unexpected journey of still being single, God gifted me with a treasure. I met a soul sister—through our blogs, of all places! Nicole "just happened" to live in the same city. (That's the hand of God, not a coincidence.) For nine months, we lived together under the same roof. By the end of our time rooming together, she was 34, and I had turned 28. One fundamental similarity in our journeys was singleness. Both of us shared a deep desire for marriage. Each of us had never, ever imagined reaching our current age and still being single. **We were living out a reality for which we had no blueprint.** This was not something we had planned or hoped for. It wasn't a possibility we had ever considered, nor had the people in our lives ever told us it could happen. Our parents were surprised that we weren't yet paired up and that they weren't grandparents. They were stepping up the prayers about our husbands.

Prolonged singleness wasn't a topic in my house growing up. It probably isn't in most households. A family member even told me, when I was just beginning my teen years, that she thought I would be married young. I went to college with dreams of a degree, and perhaps also a husband. I had heard of many couples who met during college. At first, 25 was my goal age for marriage and a baby. As I inched closer to 25, marriage was nowhere in sight. I realized it was necessary to change my expectations. I set my hopes on 28. Surely by then, I would definitely be married with a baby. That was close to 30. Life is "figured out," and dreams come true by age 30...Right? As I've matured and gained wisdom, I've realized that life is never "figured out." I'm past 28, and even past 30 now. At the time of publication, I am not "seeing" anyone. There is no ring on my finger, no baby in my arms. Before this was my reality, I simply never considered that this would be my life. I was surrounded by couples that married right after college, or even earlier. I was surrounded by families. I learned plenty about chastity and a little about healthy relationships. "Stay pure, and your marriage will be rewarded" seemed to be the message. The deep, unmet longing for marital union and a family wasn't mentioned. These talks and books never mentioned a long expedition through the winding road of singleness. My mother was married at 22. I assumed my life would follow the same trajectory. However, God's plans for our lives are often much different than we would ever dream up for ourselves.

I grew up with many people who have been married and raising families for years now. I'm still here, single, and possibly haven't even laid eyes on my husband yet. I have wondered why. Why, exactly, was this God's idea for my life? *You have a different story.* That is what the Lord has impressed upon me. No doubt, you have a different story, too! When I told a woman at a conference about the title of this book, she said with conviction: "We need different stories." As I've lived out my "different story," I have come to agree. (Though there were periods of my life when I never have believed you if you told me that I would come to a place where I would be at peace being single!)

The journey of still being single is often arduous and unexpected, yet filled to the brim with blessings. My aim is to be totally honest with you in this book. I'm not going to sweep the struggles under the rug. Throughout the writing of this book, I've experienced many stages of the single life—from near despair, to a traumatic dating experience, to joyful and hopeful expectation. I will rejoice about the blessings and share what I have learned on this sojourn. Through these insights, I hope that you might be open to what God might be inviting you to learn on this journey. I am going to challenge you out of misery and into joy. You are not alone, my friend. Won't you come along for the ride? Together, we'll board this flight and go wherever it takes us. We'll take the hand of our God and soar deeper into this journey that He has for us. I have decided to share my heart so that I can encourage you, while also trying not to sugarcoat what is often a painful reality. I pray you know you are not alone. I know how lonely this journey can feel at times. Please, be aware that you are not walking it alone; there are so many other people on the same path. You are loved and prayed for by people around the world that you do not even know.

Dear reader, I'm interceding for you as I write! Some of the things penned down in this book may be controversial for certain groups of people. There may be different ideas here than what you have been exposed to before. I aspire to follow the leading of the Holy Spirit in all I do, and these are the beliefs that I have been convicted of. I've been blessed to read a lot, meet Spirit-filled people, and have many unique life experiences. I keep it real and share different episodes from my own story throughout the book. Certain points in here may apply to just some of our stories, while others may apply to all of our stories. *Read with an open heart and a discerning spirit.* If you came across this book, I don't believe that it was random. I believe the Lord has something to say to you through it. Let the Holy Spirit speak to your heart. Whatever is resonating with you, bring it to the Lord's heart. He will use it to mold you and speak to your heart.

One last note: there are some lined journal pages in the back of the book. These are for you to write your thoughts and impressions as you read. Writing your thoughts on your "different story" is another idea. You may even step out in faith and leave them blank in order to one day write down the way that God brought about your own love story. You might want to write about how God is deepening your relationship with Him as you embrace your "different story." It's up to you. Now, let's dive in!

"But you are a chosen people, a royal priesthood, a holy nation, God's special possession, that you may declare the praises of Him who called you out of darkness into His wonderful light."
(1 Peter 2:9)

CHAPTER 1

A Peaceful Heart

$\mathcal{E}$very human being on this earth desires a heart at peace. There are numerous differences in the cultures across the globe, yet this desire is shared between all humans. Each day of our lives, we are seeking this peace. For some of us, this a journey that we are intensely aware of. Others are seeking it unconsciously and finding their efforts fall short.

The question of *how* we seek a peaceful heart is an important one. The query of what we believe will bring this peace is also crucial to consider. Perhaps, even unconsciously, we believe that marriage will bring us this peace. Having a spouse to hold and love (and to be loved by) is such a deep and strong desire. Having babies to nurture and help grow into their full potential is very appealing. These are natural and normal desires. God built us with these desires! There are definite blessings and joys associated with marriage and parenthood. Yet, if you were to obtain those things, would lasting peace be guaranteed?

"Our hearts are restless until they rest in You."[1] Written close to 1600 years ago by St. Augustine and referring to the Creator of the universe, this statement continues to hold true today, and it will throughout all time. It is imperative to know God. Where would you be without God? Take a moment to reflect on that question. You would not exist! Each of you reading has different answers for where you specifically would be without the Lord.

We can only find true peace through knowing our Creator. Our roots are from Him. Our Creator made us able to love and be loved, and we were wired to spend eternity with Him. Even if a person does not believe in God, that does not change the fact of His love for them. It does not change the fact that God created the person. Every person on the planet is seeking God. Even a person who claims not to believe in God seeks Him, though they do not believe that they are seeking Him. Even those who make decisions and get caught up with things that are opposed to the love of God want the holes of their hearts to be filled. They seek to fill the voids in their hearts with created things instead of the Creator. Ultimately, these "voids" in our lives can only be fulfilled by

---

[1] http://www.newadvent.org/fathers/ 110101.htm.

our Savior. In knowing our Creator, and not just about Him, we find balm for our seeking hearts.

No human being, career, house, bank account balance, or anything else you desire can ever meet your soul's need for the Creator. Unconsciously, a lot of singles make getting married the overarching goal of their lives. I need to break it to you: that's idolatry. Every person has idols in their life. It is easier said than done to keep God in the center of our lives. At times, we don't realize that we are seeking one thing above another. It imperceptibly becomes a part of our life through conversations, actions, and the thoughts that constantly run through our minds. It's time that we talk about idolizing marriage and a spouse. There are far too many people out there idolizing these (good) things. Though these are the good things, they are not the Good that we should be seeking overall. God is.

One Solid Foundation

It is not fair to put another person into a role that only your Creator can fill. You, and the other person, will consistently be disappointed. It's also not fair to our Creator to seek one state of life above everything else. If we're only opening our hands to one gift, we're missing out on many others. When we do so, we are missing the unique ways that the One who shapes all of history is working in our lives. We are sitting back and waiting for the greatest Artist to paint the canvas a certain way, and walking away when the first brushstrokes don't match up with what we desire the finished masterpiece to look like.

If I had married young and started having babies right away, I would have missed out on an interesting career. In my career, I've actually gained a great deal of knowledge about child development and parenting. This information will be so valuable when I finally become a parent. I am truly grateful that I didn't walk into parenthood without this knowledge. Had I married young, I probably also wouldn't have been able to achieve my dream of visiting the African continent—or it may have been deferred for a very long time. God had numerous other gifts and experiences to give me during my single years. He wanted to expand my mind and heart, and for me to learn how to relate to Him in new ways. He has revealed His love to me in bountiful ways, though those ways have not yet included a husband or sweet children. I'm immensely grateful to Him for all the ways that He has worked and continues to work in my life. Even so, I must continually seek to put Him first. The desire to be loved by and to love a man, the desire to raise children, and the desire to flourish within my career are all desires that I am aware of. Yet, I know that they are second to Jesus. Even succeeding in every one of them will not bring lasting peace.

Putting God first is a daily battle. Sometimes, it's a minute by minute and an hour by hour battle. The foundation of our relationship with God is built brick by brick, decision by decision to put Him first. Once you allow God to be in the first place of your life, the rest of your existence will fall into place. Before you seek marriage, make sure that your heart is steadfastly seeking God.

"But seek first His kingdom and His righteousness, and all these things will be given to you as well."
(Matthew 6:33)

Learn how to stand on Jesus as your Solid Rock. The only firm foundation to stand upon is Jesus Christ. There is nothing else in your life that will always be consistent. It's important for us to learn to run to Him first before we run to other people or to social media. Once you have learned to turn to your Solid Rock, you can then bring Him to others and be a solid rock for others. Your faith in the Everlasting Solid Rock will allow others to come to know Him.

The foundation that you are building now is what you will bring into a relationship and marriage. The lie that you'd be stronger and better off as a married person has swum into the minds and attitudes of numerous single people. It's a lie that I entertained for years. It's a fallacy that still tries to weave its way into my mind and heart, especially on the hard days. Life's problems don't get swept away after you've taken those marriage vows. Certain aspects of life might be smoother, but there will still be problems. You don't become a different person after making those vows and donning that wedding ring. Your last name may change, as well as details about your daily routine, but you will still be you at the very core. Any insecurities you had before will still be present during marriage. Living closely with another person and dealing with the pressures of life together will *amplify* insecurities and weaknesses. That's why it is so vital to make God your Rock now! It is so crucial to be confident in your relationship with Christ and your identity in Him. Sometimes, hasty marriages occur because people were looking to make their spouse a rock. These people, whatever their insecurities or wherever their sense of emptiness stemmed from, falsely believed that marrying would make their lives more stable. They believed that marrying this person would help solve their problems, but the realities of marriage proved otherwise. Unfortunately, I know of many marriages that ended within months or a few years. Perhaps you do, too? *A marriage must stand on and be in Christ.* The spouses must each have Christ as their Rock.[2] Before getting married, each member of the couple must be confident in their identity as a beloved child of God. Looking for stability is not a reason to get married.

I was taught that joy and contentment would follow if I have Christ as my Firm Foundation. It wasn't until I experienced this in my own life that I actually understood. It took years for this truth to move from "mind knowledge" to "heart knowledge." It's easy to do lip service to the King of kings and profess that He is your Rock. *However, is He really?* If everything were taken away, what would you do? Would you be able to cope? At the time of writing this book, there have been two horrific hurricanes, earthquakes, fires, and a worldwide pandemic. Many hearts are being sifted. We have no idea what is just around the corner and the unexpected ways that our own hearts can be sifted. I believe that even this time of longer-than-expected singleness may be a way for the Lord to sift your heart. You can allow it to bring you closer to Him, even towards that great destiny in store for your life, and to a peaceful heart filled with the joy no one can take away. Or you can allow yourself to grow bitter and resentful because your plans haven't come to fruition. The choice is yours.

---

[2] Not every marriage crumbles due to a lack of faith in one or both partners. Christians are not immune to struggles.

Coming to that place of joy and contentment in Christ is a journey. It's a constant re-working, too. As our life circumstances evolve and change, we can continue to choose Christ, or decline to continue the journey with Him. *It's truly a daily choice that we must make.* The Christian life is not half-hearted. There are numerous daily, even hourly opportunities to prove who or what we lean on.

God came to earth as a man and endured human temptations and trials. He chose to die a brutal, painful death so that we might have eternal life! Knowing this selfless, sacrificial love has made me secure. I know who I am and Whose I am. If I'm still single at the end of the day, or even until the end of my life, He is my Reason to live. *He has given me purpose and promise.* No matter the storms raging in the world or my circumstances, He is my Security—now and forever. I always have the love of Jesus to turn to. He has this in store for you, too. Take a moment to thank Him and to soak in His love.

People will come and go from our lives. Jobs will start and end. The house we are staying in now probably will not be the last home that we live in. Hold to the Rock that will never falter. No matter what happens, He will always be there.

*"Jesus Christ is the same yesterday
and today and forever."*
(Hebrews 13:8)

CHAPTER 2

No Limits

Our God is limitless. This is a truth that I've opened up my mind and heart to as the years of singleness continue to pass by. It's astounding the number of Christians who are living with a limited idea of God, expecting the way or the timing that God uses to differ from the reality of how He works. During my journey, I had to let go of many internalized ideas which were not true for my own life. I had to open my mind and heart to see the ways which the Holy Spirit was working in my life, though they were ways which were new to me.

I grew up around women who were stay-at-home mothers. In most families that I knew, the dad was the breadwinner, while the mom took care of the home and was the primary caretaker for the children. Most of these parents had married in their early twenties. I think that's one reason I struggled so much to let go of my ideal and expected timing of marriage. I had, even if unconsciously, believed that I would follow a similar track in my life. That was the reality I knew, so it's what I imagined would be true of my own life. Perhaps you, too, internalized such ideas about your future marriage, or about other areas of your life, and did not see these come to fruition.

As I lived out my twenties, the Lord continued to open my eyes to new facets of me. I discovered new ways to serve others, including avenues to minister through the written word. God unearthed dormant gifts and talents that I was created to steward. I discovered great joy in life, and on the unforeseen adventure God was leading me on.

Before I opened my eyes to God's greater vision, I limited myself to a narrow vision of getting married, being a mother, and working occasional menial jobs to support the family. Now, I have a much better picture of the calls on my life. I know now that having a family doesn't mean that I need to lose other parts of my identity. I've met or observed many women who married fairly young and got lost in motherhood, emerging later and having a crisis of sorts because they were unaware of their identities outside of being a wife and mother. I'm thankful to have realized this before entering into marriage. The other aspects of me will *enhance* my wifehood and motherhood. Because of also pouring myself into my creative gifts and to service, I'll be better able to pour into my family with joy and refreshment. Of course, there's always a balance to life. I trust that God will make that balance clear in every season.

More Than Marriage

Not everyone was created to be a spouse or a parent. For those of us who will eventually be called to marriage and parenthood, we were chosen for other roles as well. However honorable being a spouse and parent may be, they are not the *only* roles that we were destined for. What roles do you have now? How are you doing in living those with excellence? Don't limit yourself due to being single. Stop limiting yourself because society, or even the Church or its members say that you need to have someone else by your side in order to be most effective. We were created to love and be loved by our Creator and His people. Being single places no limits on that.

There is another aspect to limits, and that is limiting ourselves to certain life goals. Remember not to limit your visions and dreams to marriage. Marriage is a beautiful dream and goal, but it should not be our ultimate one. *Heaven should be.* On our way to Heaven, there is so much for us to busy ourselves in! We're called to be people of purpose and vision—to help build the Kingdom of God on earth. Holding onto the goal of marriage above all can blind you to other goals. *It distracts you from the present moment, and from serving those who have been currently placed in your life.* In fact, I believe that keeping marriage as your ultimate goal could even prevent you from meeting your spouse! Imagine if you meet your spouse while responding to one of the calls God has placed upon your life? Or imagine connecting with someone due to shared visions for the future? Your mate will enhance your dreams and callings. Your mate will be your biggest cheerleader and enable you to shine even more brightly in whatever callings you have in your life.

Ask your Heavenly Father for the dreams that He has for you. Each one of us was created to dream and to live out these dreams, partnering with God to do beautiful things on this earth. Dream big! Don't wait to dream because you're single. Now is the time to start dreaming those dreams which God has birthed deep in your heart.

There are those who will enter into marriage with the expanded vision of their lives and callings. Others will discover these callings later on as they live out the calling of marriage. I believe that God intends for us to be with spouses that will be our greatest encouragers in *all* of our callings. A great spouse will be your greatest fan in whatever you are called to do in this world. They will be someone who draws you to become the best version of yourself. On the days when you have difficulty believing in yourself, your spouse will be the one to remind you that you are a conqueror in Jesus Christ. Your spouse will need to be a person who helps you to carry what you've been given to bless this world with. You, in turn, will be tasked with helping them to bear the calls which are upon their life.

In any area of your life, stop limiting yourself! Your thought patterns may be holding you back from accomplishing great things, and from growing into the person your Creator intended for you to be. Sometimes, the greatest limits in our lives are the ones that we place on ourselves. Do you realize that many of us also put God in a box, expecting that He will definitely work in a certain way? Don't limit Him, even in your mind! **The Lord has absolutely no limits on how, when, and where He works!** In every aspect of our lives, God is creative! There are no limits on the way He works, even if people have tried to limit God's ways. When we expect God to absolutely work in a certain way or using a certain formula, it can prevent us from seeing the reality of how God is actually working or intending to work in a situation.

There are people who expect to definitely meet their spouse in a certain location or a specific way. It's time that we also let go of these limits which we've imposed in our minds. There are "traditional" ways of meeting someone, but there are also many new and unexpected ways. Every love story is a different story! God cannot be put into a box. To place limits and constraints on the way God works is a great dishonor to the One Who cannot be contained.

> *"Oh, the depth of the riches of the wisdom and knowledge of God! How unsearchable His judgments, and His paths beyond tracing out!"*
> *(Romans 11:33)*

Living in purpose can help with the waiting period. However, it can be challenging if you know that your spouse will complement your purpose and enable you to be stronger in it. We all want someone by our side to acknowledge how far we've come, and to run with us to where we are going. Stay strong and trust in God's perfect timing. It's up to God's perfect timing to decide when the two journeys will merge. It will make more sense *why* we waited so long when we discover the path which the other person traversed and compare the two paths. This is what I believe.

"Before I formed you in the womb I knew you, before you were born I set you apart; I appointed you as a prophet to the nations." (Jeremiah 1:5)

Open your heart to the plan that your Creator has for you. I know that it's frustrating to hold tightly to a blueprint, only to watch it crumble in front of your eyes. The crumbling of that blueprint is an opportunity for us to widen our vision. It is a time for us to let go and allow the Master Architect to build our lives. He can do so much better than we can! In Him, we are limitless! Let's intercede for the grace of seeing ourselves the way that our Heavenly Father does. Press in for His expansive vision for your life. As His vision for you is revealed, you might be amazed at the ways that you are holding yourself back from letting your light shine! The ways that you are even placing limits upon Him may also come to light.

Know that your Heavenly Father is smiling upon you as you begin to live out the dreams that He envisioned for you before you were even in your mother's womb. **Praise be to You, our limitless and all-seeing Lord!**

"Do not conform to the pattern of this world, but be transformed by the renewing of your mind. Then you will be able to test and approve what God's will is—His good, pleasing and perfect will." (Romans 12:2)

CHAPTER 3

On Jealousy and the Journey

Have you ever struggled with jealousy or envy? If you're reading this book, my guess is that you have. You've watched from the sidelines as yet *another* relationship progresses to engagement and a wedding. There you are, still by yourself. Then, there is a baby announcement. Your heart explodes with love for that little one, though you can't help but ache for when you'll finally hold *your* bundle of joy. You begin to feel left out as friends and acquaintances pair up, stay together, and create families of their own. Sometimes, it can be tempting to ask God, *"why?"* At other times, we wonder if our Heavenly Father is even listening. Take comfort as you read the following Bible verse:

> *"But God has surely listened and has heard my prayer. Praise be to God, Who has not rejected my prayer or withheld His love from me!" (Psalm 66:19-20)*

It is imperative to let go of jealousy. I know that this is often easier said than done. Remember, *your* story is not their story. Your story *cannot* and *will not* compare to another person's story. Though it can be painful to still be the one waiting, it's important to remember that God is working individually in each of our lives. He cares about us corporately, as well as individually, in ways that we can't even comprehend. We have no idea what, exactly, is happening behind the scenes. We don't know the amazing ways that God is lining up our lives to bring our spouse to us or to reveal us to each other. Overall, we don't know the wonderful blessings and gifts that the Master Weaver of our lives has in store.

Comparison: A Thief

We wonder about other people's stories and compare them to ours. Why do their prayers get answered so quickly? How can an 18-year old pray one fervent prayer and meet their spouse twenty minutes after joining CatholicMatch or

ChristianMingle? Why do some people pray and fast for years, even decades, and endure countless heartbreaks—with still no spouse in sight? Why are some people who are so generous and giving, and with such strong desires for marriage and parenthood, still on the sidelines? It can be difficult not to wonder why some of us are asked to traipse through this wearisome journey of life without a partner for so long, while others meet their life partner at a young age. I can't completely answer these difficult questions or explain these differences between stories. I do know that God holds every story in esteem. Each story is important to Him. I can also tell you that this world holds immense brokenness. God holds a view of all of history, which we cannot see. Somehow, He is working together all of this for our good and the good of future generations.

I remember when I was a kid, and my dad would blast music in the family room with his big speakers from the 80's. We, the kiddos, would dance and burn off some of our seemingly unending energy. One song which was seared in my memory is "God Is In Control" by Twila Paris. As a child, I could never have imagined how much the song would mean to me over twenty years later. Even on the days when I don't understand what's going on in my life and the world, and how it could be worked for good, I know: God is in control. We can rest in that fact. Don't let comparison rob you of the joy to be found in your "different story."

Focus on Your Journey

We must learn to trust the journey that the Lord has given us, and trust others with what they have been given. Focus on enjoying your own journey. Forget what people think when it comes to the unique path which you've been given to walk out. They can't understand, because it's a journey that they themselves were not chosen for. Don't judge their journey or yours. Every assigned path is a Divine masterpiece in progress.

I remember a road trip where I noticed a "bubble" on one of my tires. Realizing the dangers of continuing the trip, I decided to replace the "bubble" tire with a spare tire. I still had two hours of driving before I would reach home. If you know anything about the small spare tires that come with a car, you know that extra attention must be paid to your speed. It is dangerous to go too fast. For the remainder of the trip (which would now definitely take more than two hours), I poked along in the right lane while other vehicles sped by. Some of the other drivers gave me dirty looks as they passed. *Yet, they didn't know what I knew. They didn't see what I saw.* Our Heavenly Father sees the entire picture of our lives. He understands that He could be keeping us from an inevitable disaster by *not* getting married, just as I realized that driving beyond the speed limit with that small tire could have kept me from a bad accident. As I moseyed along at a much slower pace than I would have ever desired, I saw interesting and beautiful sights. That road trip is one that I had made numerous times before. However, I had never seen the things I saw that day because I had been going so fast before! I believe that a time of extended singleness gives us time and perspective to see things we wouldn't see otherwise.

We are given time for the Lord to reveal our true hearts. Our character is revealed, and extra time is given to chip away at our flaws. We see our strengths and the gifts that God is asking us to use in the world. Marriage is like a mirror, or so I've heard numerous married couples say. For those of us who will be married one day, we'll go through even greater refining as we live out the marriage covenant and raise small human beings.

Let's learn to appreciate and even love the beauty and differences between our story and the stories of others. Perhaps when your love is standing before you, it will make more sense and be easier to do so. I believe that it will, and you'll see God's hand as you get to know the person and the interweaving of your life stories.

Being single could make you bitter. It could turn you to jealousy and resentment. On the other hand, it could open you to awe of God's wondrous plan and care for the details of your life. If you allow it, it can change your focus to His amazing, wonderful, and unique ways in each of our lives. Cling to faith and trust; let go of jealousy. Jealousy won't draw you any closer to God's great plans for you. It will only destroy you and distract you from focusing on your unrepeatable journey. Choose trust and joy over jealousy.

CHAPTER 4

Against Discouragement

There is a word that we need to talk about and to battle against if it comes anywhere near us. That word is *discouragement.* I know how difficult it can be not to get discouraged, friends. It's something I still battle occasionally. When you see people a decade (or more) younger than yourself getting married and becoming parents—it can be discouraging. It can make one wonder what in the world God is doing. You might feel forgotten by God. When, yet again, "talking" turns to disappointment—it is discouraging. When in a dating situation which seems to be headed toward the altar, and then finding out about huge secrets or unfaithfulness—it is absolutely discouraging! I am sure you have experienced other immensely discouraging scenarios as well. It's essential to have people you can be vulnerable with and share your discouragements with.

However, they need to be people that will encourage you in the end. Flee from people who *discourage* you. These individuals do not have your best interests at heart.

When discouragement comes in, it's easy to want to shut down. My single sisters and I could tell you so many stories! We've had experiences where men presented their character as being quite the opposite of what they really stood for. Those instances of finding out a person's true colors can be immensely disappointing. Dating an amazing man and beginning to realize that you could marry him, and then being dumped, can turn your world upside down. Meeting a woman who seems to be an answer to your prayers, and then being rejected when you want to date her, is discouraging. In any of these instances or the ones that you have experienced, it can be hard to trust or open up again. Just thinking about starting the process and the possibility of going through it afresh can be exhausting.

"Endure hardship as discipline; God is treating you as his children. For what children are not disciplined by their father? If you are not disciplined—and everyone undergoes discipline—then you are not legitimate, not true sons and daughters at all. Moreover, we have all had human fathers who

disciplined us and we respected them for it.
How much more should we submit to the
Father of spirits and live! They disciplined us
for a little while as they thought best; but God
disciplines us for our good, in order that we
may share in His holiness. No discipline seems
pleasant at the time, but painful. Later on,
however, it produces a harvest of
righteousness and peace for those who have
been trained by it."
(Hebrews 12:7-11)

Sowing and Reaping

There have been times on this journey of singleness when I wanted to throw in the towel. I know, that's not really possible-you can't go to the store or log in to Amazon and pick out your God-given spouse! There is often the temptation to believe that life would be easier-i*f only I were married.* Years of singleness when I had never imagined still being single is *tiring*, especially when I allow the I-can't-do-it-anymore attitude to creep in. The truth is, we are so much stronger than we could ever imagine! We have the Creator and Savior of the world on our side. Learning to soak my mind into the Word of God has been immensely helpful to me. Scripture has strengthened me and provided wisdom and clearer understanding. The above passage from the Book of Hebrews encourages me that this is not in vain. As verse 11 says, discipline does not seem pleasant, but painful. Yet, this discipline is a share in God's holiness! It will later produce a harvest of righteousness and peace. Isn't that beautiful? I will compare being single for an extended time as parallel to a barren field. Yet later, the field will be abundant with the harvest, so much so that you can barely collect all its fruits! I believe that those who are faithful to God in waiting for His timing will have an abundant harvest, both for themselves and their families, in the current and future generations.

During the period of sowing, so much can happen. Hopes and dreams build up. Eventually, you might meet a person that awakens your hope in a refreshing way. You're filled with awe, having waited to meet a person like them for *so long*. You talk for hours together. The feeling seems to be mutual, and maybe it even is. But then comes the moment when it all comes crashing down. It might happen a few weeks after you've met them. It could also occur months into a relationship with them, when you realize with stunning clarity that he (or she) is not "the one" for you. Maybe there were lots of little moments which culminated into this big moment. Perhaps it is the other person who has the dreaded conversation with you, informing you that the feeling is not mutual. It won't work out between you the two of you. Disappointment comes in once again.

Those moments of realization that it's not going to work out with a particular individual are painful. Once again, it's time to start all over with someone else. It could be years before that happens. "What's your name?" "What's your story?" "Where are you from?" "Tell me about your family." From the ground up, you will need to begin again, when the time comes. The process is not easy, but it's an element of this life's journey. We must submit to it, because no blessing is built up overnight.

On Continuous Disappointments

> "Hope deferred makes the heart
> sick, but a longing fulfilled is a tree
> of life." (Proverbs 13:12)

Continuous disappointments can really weigh on a person. Even the Bible tells us so in the scripture above. As a person who has been unmarried for years longer than I expected, I've had to realize the weight of these disappointments. A lot of disappointments can transpire even within a short period. These disappointments can relate to the opposite sex, but they can also occur in other areas of our lives. As I write this chapter, I realized a deeper meaning to the word "disappointment." Upon meeting a new person, or as friendship develops, you begin to believe that you and that person have an appointment with destiny. When it turns out that there is not an appointment with destiny in regards to that particular person, it's a crushing experience. When these disappointing experiences happen in other areas of our lives, it can be very painful. Be assured that, no matter how many disappointments you've endured, God has astonishing appointments confirmed for your future!

Disappointment has to be one of the deepest pains of this life. Words can't adequately describe the hurt. You may have lived through the experience of disappointment many times over and not need any words written on this page to describe it for you. Disappointments hurt, but they can allow us to grow and better prepare to receive for what is in store for us.

Seek not to brush your disappointments under the rug. Acknowledge them and give them to God. Cry it out. It's okay to allow yourself that release. In fact, it's actually healthy. Talk about your disappointments to trusted friends. Journaling can also be a helpful tool. If it really weighs on you, going to therapy and talking about it with an objective person can also be healing and cathartic. I've cried many tears, written many journal entries, and had countless conversations about this topic. We need to bring these things to light instead of suppressing them. There's no use in trying to suppress because these things will still come out in other forms. Often, they will show themselves at an inopportune time. Our emotions are normal, and there is no need to be ashamed of them. They are there, so allow them to come to light so that they can be addressed in a healthy manner.

When you are feeling low about your single state, aching for your spouse, or even fearful that you'll never be married, bring it to Jesus. Don't let yourself even for a second sink down into doubts. The Evil One wants us to stay in misery. The forces working against us desire for us to sink lower into the abyss of negativity. Once you've allowed yourself to sink into it, this mire is not easy to climb out of. Acknowledge the way you are feeling and why you are feeling that way. Then, talk with Jesus and allow Him to transform those areas of your heart.

"In your anger do not sin": Do not let the sun go down while you are still angry, and do not give the devil a foothold."
(Ephesians 4:26-27)

I've cried countless tears about my single state. Our emotions are valid, and it's unhealthy to suppress them. It is totally normal to feel a sense of loss, to grieve, and to feel sadness. Yet, I wish that some of those nights I spent crying would have been spent more productively, instead of letting myself sink into a deeper abyss of sadness. I used unhealthy ways to cope with loneliness, which ended up making loneliness even more apparent. Though it's normal to cry and express our emotions, I wish I wouldn't have let myself wallow as much as I did. My desire became selfish. There are people all over this world crying for much more pressing reasons than the lack of a husband. I wish I could have dwelt more fully on the goodness of God during those seasons, and focused on spreading His love.

> *'The thief comes only to steal and kill and destroy; I have come that they may have life, and have it to the full." (John 10:10)*

One of the reasons our Amazing Savior came to earth is so that we could live life to the fullest. Of course, this ultimately means our salvation and living eternally! Yet, in this life too, there is so much fullness and abundance. A full life is *not* dependent on a significant other or marriage. We are called and equipped to live in joy. It doesn't matter whether you are single, dating, engaged, or married—there will never be perfect circumstances in your life. We must find joy. In Jesus, we learn to live in joy and abundance. Ask Him to teach you to live this way.

Don't allow bitterness or resentment to take root. I know it can be very difficult not to. That's why you need to address it as soon as it is brought to your attention (whether by yourself or by someone else). There were months, even years, when I was angry at God. I blamed the problems in my life on being single. In turn, I blamed God that I was single. The Lord has done so much healing in me since those days. I don't carry that anger anymore. There is purpose and meaning in singleness. The gifts in this season are much more clear to me. You can be healed, too, if you allow yourself to turn from bitterness and run to the waiting arms of your Heavenly Father.

I am learning to look at each disappointment through the lens of *encouragement.* When a lack of character is revealed, or the Holy Spirit is not giving me peace, I'm learning to cling to my Heavenly Father and His perfect plan. Letting go means that I'm free to pick up other gifts, and to one day receive the person that Jehovah does have for me. Even these bumps on the road are purposeful. Throw away disappointment and kick discouragement to the curb. Choose instead to live with hope.

CHAPTER 5

Let's Talk Genealogy

P eople want to know who they are. Myriads of people in America are sending in their saliva to get their DNA tested and figure out where they came from. Roots are important because they establish us. They connect us to others and to God. Genealogy is important to God. Just think about the Bible. Salvation history is based upon a family line. Both the Old and New Testaments list long genealogies. The story of Jesus wouldn't make sense without all the figures and stories that came before and next to Him.

No one reading this came into existence without others. Each of us came from a family that has existed for centuries. Over time, much has happened within each of our families. Patterns have been made and continued throughout generations. Predispositions have been formed within our DNA. Generational curses have been passed down. Generational *blessings* have also been passed down.

Marriage Matters to God

It *does* matter to God whom you marry. Your specific marriage will have a tremendous impact on the course of your life, and even on history. It is true that we have free will. That free will extends to our choice in marriage partner. Though we have free will in choosing, I *do* believe that we can choose to wait for the suitable partner that God has for us. As Scripture tells us, our Heavenly Father cares about the sparrows. If He cares so deeply about the sparrows, He definitely cares about who you marry and commit your entire life to!

"Are not two sparrows sold for a penny? Yet not one of them will fall to the ground outside your Father's care. And even the very hairs of your head are all numbered. So don't be afraid; you are worth more than many sparrows." (Matthew 10:29-31)

We are so valuable to our Heavenly Father! The details of our lives are important to Him. Think about the level of detail which you have experienced in other aspects of your life, from the people God has placed in your life, the jobs He has helped you to obtain, and all the little ways He reveals His specific love toward you each day. If God cares about all of those details, how much more does He delight in bringing you a spouse suitable for you and to be a parent to your future (and current) children? Our Heavenly Father is a good Father, and these details of our lives are definitely significant to Him.

"Which of you, if your son asks for bread, will give him a stone? Or if he asks for a fish, will give him a snake? If you, then, though you are evil, know how to give good gifts to your children, how much more will your Father in heaven give good gifts to those who ask Him!"
(Matthew 7:9-11)

My father told me a story that hit home for me about the topic of Divine intervention in regard to a life partner. There was a girl he had been interested in for about a year. Then, one life-changing day, he met my mother. My father and mother began dating. Right around this time, the other girl that he had been interested in decided that she was ready to date my dad! What if he had ended up with her instead of my mom? My siblings and I wouldn't exist! Most importantly, my father discovered a deeper faith through my mom. Faith may not have been part of our heritage, had he ended up with the other woman. What a cherished part of my heritage it is, one that I'll pass on to my children with much reverence. I pray that they see the richness of this treasure and pass it along to their offspring also.

Your marriage and the way you parent with your spouse will impart beliefs and attitudes to your children. When you spend time with a potential spouse, look for what their words and actions communicate to you and those around them. This will give you a hint into how they will nurture and build up any children or people placed into your lives. It might reveal to you that they are actually a person who does more to break people down than to build them up. Watch for these indications, and be cautious about proceeding if what they are sowing into the world now doesn't match with what you envision for the world's future.

He's Intentional

I heard a talk from a counselor and prophetess who is well-acquainted with equipping singles and couples for marriage, as well as counseling married people.[3] One of the points that she made is that God is thinking about our DNA when it comes to who we are attracted to. The Father's design is so intricate! Even the way that He has made our biology and caused us to be attracted to one another is so purposeful. The DNA that we pass along to children will continue to affect generations long after we have moved on from this earth. It's remarkable to think about how our choice will affect generations that we may never meet on this side of Heaven. What responsibility we have as children of God!

While God may have "wired" us to be attracted to certain types of people, we must also be mindful. Some of you have patterns where you are attracted to those who don't inspire you to be the best of yourself. Some of you discover that those who are attracted to you simply aren't seeking to live a godly lifestyle. Figure out what's attracting you to those types of people. Or, what is it that attracts them to you? Are you attracted to men like your father, unconsciously wanting to make "right" what was twisted in your childhood? Are you attracted to women that demean you and your self-esteem, providing you familiarity with what you've known before? Think and pray very carefully about the type of person you want to attract and be attracted to, and why these attractions are happening. Write down these patterns that you want

---

[3] http://www.askdoctorfaith.com

broken and pray over them. Think about concrete ways to stop these patterns. Sometimes, counseling can be a helpful tool to gain an objective perspective.

I believe that God's care of who we marry is one reason it may take so long for two people to end up together. Our Creator is refining our future spouses and us. This process of refinement will continue for the rest of our lives. There are some of us that He allows to receive a bit more polishing before we are ready to be married. For whatever reason, other couples are polished from a young age as they journey together. For those of us waiting longer to be married, the journey of our lives may take longer for us to end up in the same place, readiness-wise and even geographically.

Observe and Discern

Looking at familial patterns should be an urgent priority when you are considering a potential spouse. If you can get to know the person's family, that is a huge blessing. You will be able to observe the family's patterns of relating and behaving. You will be able to sense if you are accepted into that family. If it's difficult to imagine being a part of that family, pause and step back. You marry an individual, but you are marrying into a family. They will become a significant part of your life and your children's lives. If members of your family or a potential spouse's family are prone to certain behaviors or addictions, your children will very likely also have a propensity to those things. Some people have chosen to distance themselves from their families due to dysfunction and choosing to live in a healthier way. Listen for this in conversations with the potential spouse. It's crucial to address these issues through prayer, honest conversations, and counseling. Seek deliverance from generational bondage and patterns. Future generations will thank you. Marriage affects so much more than the two people standing at the altar making vows to one another. Marriage affects communities and future generations.

I'm not suggesting that you should reconsider someone based on one concern. We all have deal-breakers, and there are red flags to look out for, but grace is also readily available. No human being is perfect. No family is perfect. However, it is crucial to think about the offspring of this particular person and how they could be affected by these generational patterns. You also need to know what you are looking for in a spouse, and what you definitely want to avoid. It's important to make sure that you are on the same page with a potential spouse about what you desire to instill in your future family and the world. *You must make these decisions under the continued guidance of the Holy Spirit.* It's so vital to have wise, Holy Spirit-filled individuals in our lives, to speak truth and wisdom to us! Again, we also remember that there is *always* grace. With Jesus, any curse can be broken. Any disease can be healed, and any behavior pattern changed. Hallelujah!

This topic can be a difficult one. We live in an incredibly broken world. No family is perfect, and no person is perfect. Each one of us will marry a human being with flaws and weaknesses. Yet, you don't need to follow the negative patterns which your ancestors or family members followed. Because your grandmother and mother married an alcoholic, that does not mean that you also need to marry an alcoholic. I'm sure you can think of examples specific to your family situation. You can make the choice for your family to be the one to start the healing process for your bloodline and ensure that future generations will live in greater freedom than the ones before.

Pay attention to what the Holy Spirit tells you in prayer. Hearken to the wisdom shared with you by those you trust. Don't neglect the difficult conversations. Observe how the person has been able to cooperate with grace on their life journey so far. Talk about the positive changes that each of you have made in your lives. Discuss your dreams for the future. Make your decision wisely, and never cease praying for your spouse, your children (or future children), and for your families. Leave the rest to God.

CHAPTER 6

Where is The Church?

ere you taught that waiting on the Lord for a spouse could take decades? *I will tell you, I sure wasn't!* At different church-sponsored events, I heard plenty about abstinence, chastity, and the fruit it would bring to a marriage. As a teen, I heard numerous talks on this topic. A demonstration of this subject was made, where two pieces of construction paper were glued together. When the speaker tried to take them apart, portions of one paper stuck to the other. The message got across that sex was something sacred and that you can't have sex with someone without consequences. I signed a pledge to wait for my husband when I was 15 years old. I was never advised that a husband might not come along until much later. I don't remember hearing advice about what it takes to build healthy relationships. Somehow it seemed to be assumed that marriages just fell into place! At the time, I was surrounded by people who were married directly after college, during college, or even soon after high school. Within these abstinence talks, strategies for staying pure weren't even talked about. The message was basically: Wait. Abstain.

Besides chastity, there are many other facets that go into building thriving marriages and healthy parent-child relationships. I believe that it's time the Church puts methods into place to holistically teach the next generation about marriage and family life—all of it. Maybe one of you reading will create mind-blowing programs to do so! Some of you reading are going to be part of a couple that will powerfully reveal God's plan for marriage to the world. Example: the best way of teaching!

It's time for the members of the Body of Christ to be realistic about the situation in the present time. Purity is timeless and non-negotiable. Yet, as a foundation, youth must be taught to keep their eyes on Jesus, first and foremost. Following God's specific will for you should also be a lesson. Youth need to be taught the building blocks for healthy relationships, as well as live among examples of these relationships. The media, as well as the reality which youth are growing up in, often don't depict functional, healthy relationships.

It's also time for the Church to grasp that meeting a suitable spouse is not as simple as it may have been in the past. Youth need to find a strong identity in Christ most of all, and be encouraged to live in purpose and service. When youth reach adulthood, they then see that most events and groups at churches are aimed at families. While I think there has been improvement in catering to singles, there is also still a long way to go. Even having programs that are open to each marital status and age group could be a good idea. Each stage and state of life have much to learn from each other.

A New Calling

This is a new generation. Your parents likely didn't see too many people single into their late twenties, thirties, forties, or even later. Finding a person of character who is also suitable for you is much more difficult presently than in previous generations. The times are different, and godly character isn't quite so common anymore. The path to marriage for modern couples is often more difficult due to the problems within society that even members of the Church are not immune from.

Growing up in the Church, I internalized an unhealthy narrative of life which I had to let go of. I know that I'm the only one who picked up on this idea. This narrative, even if not explicitly taught, gave me the idea that it is better to marry early, and the more kids you have, the better. These ideas are damaging, because they promote the idea that one narrative is better than another. When this narrative turns out to be far from the reality of a person's life, they may believe that something is wrong with them. In reality, God simply had another path for that person. Again, God is not limited to one narrative! Every member of the Church has a different story. Every story teaches us and shows us the light of Christ in a different way.

In many respects, members of the Church do not understand the great cross that extended singleness is. Older members especially may not have seen this cross lived out. They may even blame the person who is carrying it. People are told they need to do more, or that they are doing something wrong, or just need to settle down and make up their mind. Unfortunately, there is even the idea (if not uttered aloud, it is implied) that a single person is "less than." I've read articles where it is inferred that a Christian person called to the married life must make living their vocation their main goal. The insinuation is that a single person is basically in control of finding a spouse. I think that could also be considered idolatry, or playing God. I want to marry the person that God has called me to be with, not simply to marry someone for the sake of living a vocation. Don't let someone else's ideas rush you into a premature marriage. Don't let another person's (possibly misguided) opinions change how you feel about yourself. Keep your eyes focused on Christ and His perfect plan for your life.

"Those who look to Him are radiant; their faces are never covered with shame."
(Psalm 34:5)

I don't know if something will change in the next generation which will turn the tide and make finding a holy spouse easier. There is so much within society and the Church that will need to change for that to happen. Perhaps we are the examples for the next generation. Faithfully, we will live out singleness and the other specific calls we have been entrusted with. If this long desert of singleness is a call that others will also be asked to take up in the future, we are the testimony. It *can* be done. Our gracious Heavenly Father will provide the grace we need to walk out the calls He has given to each one of us.

'Three times I pleaded with the Lord to take it away from me. But He said to me, "My grace is sufficient for you, for my power is

> *made perfect in weakness."*
> *Therefore I will boast all the more*
> *gladly about my weaknesses, so that*
> *Christ's power may rest on me." (2*
> *Corinthians 12:8-9)*

Friends, we're charting new territory. What an enormous responsibility for us! Yet, what a blessing and relief for the next generation. Perhaps because of our faithfulness to this call and sharing the wisdom we gained, their cross might be a little lighter to bear. I'm not exactly sure why you and I have been chosen for this, but I pray that we steward the call well. It is often a difficult call to live out, and one that doesn't humanly make sense. But I believe that it is not without purpose. There is meaning in making and walking on a new path. As Robert Frost wrote, "I took the one less traveled by, and that has made all the difference."[4]

There is more to life than marriage. Somehow, it seems that pockets in Christianity have made an idol of marriage. The theology of Christ and the Church and how marriage reflects this relationship to the world is beautiful. It's a gift to be able to live that out. Yet, read and reflect on St. Paul's writings to the Corinthians regarding singleness.[5] Think

---

[4] https://www.poetryfoundation.org/poems/44272/the-road-not-taken.
[5] 1 Corinthians 7

about the people in the Bible who were not married. *Jesus* was not married! The Church needs to find ways to affirm those who are serving the Church as single people. Members of the Church must find ways to welcome and accept singles into their community. The members of Christ's body must also learn to accept those living a different life stage reality and timing than they are accustomed to seeing. Each one must learn to affirm the others. Singles, we also must recognize our own attitudes. For example, we need to stop being jealous of those living the married life or becoming parents. We need to remember that people living out the married state of life most definitely still have crosses to bear. As Christians, we are also called to intercede for them and to serve them however we are able. As I mentioned before, singleness even provides more freedom to serve! Though we're praying for marriage, we might be the answer to prayer for a struggling mom or family in need of some extra help or community.

It can be difficult to be a single in the Church. There are those whose attitudes can make it more difficult. Yet we also need to be compassionate to those who are not kind or understanding to us as singles. I pray that the Church is willing to hear our "different stories." The Body of Christ must understand and support us on the journeys that we have been tasked to undertake. We, too, must support them in their vocation and journey. Each member of the Body is tasked with faithfulness to fulfilling their current function. The Body of Christ will only shine brighter as we all begin to embrace and focus upon our specific and unique stories.

CHAPTER 7

A Different Calling

The desire to be with another person and build a family is natural. Shouldn't it fall into place easily? I've wondered the same thing—so have many of my single sisters. Perhaps you single brothers have had the same question. For the people of many generations, finding a spouse was simple. The majority of people were married rather early in life. Now, here we are, single at an age where we never expected to be. It may feel unacceptable to you or the people in your life that you are single. Different stories are often misunderstood. Sometimes, different stories are hated. Society has a way of conditioning us to expect a certain story to play out in our lives, and making us feel strange when that script doesn't play out. Our "different stories" can even feel burdensome to us. The fact is, we are set apart. *We are living a different calling.* Sometimes, God calls us to the supernatural, and He gives us the grace to walk it out. We learn that we can only lean on Him in order to do so.

"I have given them Your word and the world has hated them, for they are not of the world any more than I am of the world. My prayer is not that You take them out of the world but that You protect them from the evil one. They are not of the world, even as I am not of it. Sanctify them by the truth; Your word is truth. As You sent me into the world, I have sent them into the world." (John 17:14-18)

Your different calling is benefitting and will benefit this world in ways that you could never have dreamed up! This world cries out under the suffering of humanity. There are more types of suffering than we can even imagine. The good news is that we were created for such a time as this! You were created by God to impact this world, and the eternal lives of others, in a deep way. Your different calling is vital! People are waiting for you to step out and live the destiny that God has for you. Only you can do this, in partnership with the One who created you. There is not any other person in history who can make exactly the mark which God has called you to make!

---

*"For the creation waits in eager
expectation for the children of God
to be revealed."
(Romans 8:19)*

Freedom and Singleness

You don't need to be married to offer your unique gifts. In some cases, being single will provide *more* freedom for you to minister with these gifts. Singleness often provides more availability than the married state does. Every day, ask the Holy Spirit what mission you are being asked to live, and who you are being called to love. The Spirit-led life is such an adventure! I promise that your different calling, your different story, will never allow you to taste boredom!

Appreciate the beauty and difference between your story and the stories of others. Just think, no one in history will ever have an account exactly the same as yours! A friend of mine gave a word about there being many "Noahs," called to do something that has never been done before. If you're reading this book, I believe that you have been chosen to be one of those Noahs. What ark have you been called to build with your life? You're building something which will continue on even after you have left this earth. If you truly don't know what your purpose is, pray into it. The Lord will reveal it to you in various ways. Perhaps He has already begun that process of revelation in your life.

I wonder what needs the Lord has specifically equipped you to fill with the precious, available time that He has gifted you? Maybe it's building a closer relationship with that neighbor that you've become more friendly with. In doing so, perhaps the door has opened for you to be able to share your testimony and lead them to Christ. Maybe the local homeless shelter is looking for someone to create fun activities for the kids so that they can simply be children and play instead of having the weight of the world on their shoulders. If you're reading this, you are a world-changer! I am so excited for you to continue walking into the great things that God has prepared for you! I'm anticipating the ways that the world will be a more loving, Christ-centered place because of you.

"For we are God's handiwork, created in Christ Jesus to do good works, which God prepared in advance for us to do." (Ephesians 2:10)

Some of you reading are already living out your "different calling" with great fervor. May the Lord continue to grace you with strength and endurance to do so! Other readers are still unsure of what their unique calling(s) are. Whatever your unique and special calling may be, I pray that the Lord will reveal it to you. Have courage that He will provide the grace for you to live it out. While you live out your season of extended singleness, may you be relentless in your pursuit of the purpose that God has laid upon your heart! May that relentless pursuit lead you to a lifetime of flourishing in your "different story."

Love Your Story and Calling

Learn to love your story. Love the calling that you have been specially entrusted with. It may look very different than you imagined, *perhaps* nothing like you ever imagined. The way the Lord works in my life will likely differ from the way He works in yours. Comparing our stories is futile. Think about the Bible. The Book of Genesis and the Book of Luke are each part of salvation history. However, each book tells a very different part of the story. Each fulfills a distinct purpose in our understanding of salvation and our relation to God. Each of us is a different part of the Body of Christ and performs a different function. Doesn't it make sense, then, that none of our stories is exactly alike? What an uninteresting world it would be if all of us had the same story. I'm so grateful that the Lord writes a different book with each of our stories! This adds such a richness to the Church and the world.

"Just as a body, though one, has many parts, but all its many parts form one body, so it is with Christ."
(1 Corinthians 12:12)

There are hindrances that can lead to difficulty accepting and loving your story. These hindrances can lead people to want to fulfill a different role that was never theirs to fill. Social media is one prominent mechanism that leads many people to compare themselves to others. Comparison is unrealistic and in vain. It is toxic and feeds the people comparing themselves lies about themselves and their worth. Social media presents an illusion. People post the highlights of their lives. Pictures are doctored up to look perfect, hiding any messiness. People show the highlights and mountaintop moments—or at least the pictures present these moments to be such. Generally speaking, struggles are filtered out on social media. Social media has become such a facet in many people's lives that they often don't even realize how it could be negatively impacting them or leading to comparison.

It's unnecessary to compare ourselves to others. Why compare a rose to an orchid? They are different and yet both beautiful, each adding different colors and textures to the garden. Your different story is needed. No one's story is better or more desirable for you than your very own!

Your story is a great one! Your story can inspire others. No one else in all of history has had your exact story. No one in the future will share your exact story. However, living a different calling than society expects (and even the Church, sometimes) has its share of difficulties. Bring it to God when you struggle with your story. He Who gave you the very gift of life is ready to encourage and walk with you as you live the story crafted especially for you!

CHAPTER 8

Divine Protection

*D*id you ever think that perhaps your current single state could be *protecting* you? I think that this could be the case for many singles. Too many people marry without seeking God about the matter first. Sometimes, they rush into a marriage without knowing crucial details about their spouse. They may have married because of societal or familial pressure. At a certain point, some people simply get so tired that they settle and get married due to feeling like it is time to do so.

Singleness as a Shield

As painful as the sufferings of singleness can be, it sobers me when I perceive it could be shielding me from other potential sufferings. There are so many men and women in marriages that they wish they could get out of. The pain of singleness may be shielding you from financial trouble that another person (maybe secretly) brought into the marriage. It might be shielding you from emotional abuse by a spouse, or intimate partner violence. You could be protected from deception, from secrets that hurt and that the person you love decided to hide from you. You could be protected from another person's harmful addiction. Being single might be protecting you from a man (or woman) who is adulterous and later leaves you and your children. Singleness keeps you from a lifetime of feeling stuck with someone who isn't suitable for you. The list could go on and on. Only God knows what you *specifically* are being protected from in your current state. Marriage will contain its own unique suffering. Don't be quick to exchange this cross for a different one.

Count your current singleness as a hand of protection over your life and your future marriage and children. I've heard it said that "rejection is God's protection." What powerful truth is packed in that short statement! Though you may have desperately wanted to end up with a certain person, you don't know what God can see that you don't. This period of singleness is providing wisdom for you to choose a suitable partner for you and to let go of those who are not ideal for you.

At one point, I had been in a relationship for about a year. He was a man with many positive character qualities. It was a great relationship, and he treated me well. We had many common goals for the future, which was not easy for me to find in other men. Yet, I never felt quite settled or totally at peace. I lacked joy and peace when I thought and prayed about marrying him. I even had dreams where it was our wedding day, but I could not go through with the marriage. I sought counsel often and from many people, but my heart never resonated with the idea of marrying him. Peace and joy never followed my prayer or conversations about our potential marriage. It became clear that God was asking me to let go of the relationship. By the grace of God, I found the strength to break it off. It is years past that relationship now. Our lives went in different directions. Now, I have a clearer perspective of why God asked me to let go of that relationship. That young man was shielded from me! I was also shielded from certain circumstances that would have been totally unnecessary for my life. These circumstances would have kept me from achieving or beginning to follow certain callings in my life. By a miracle of God, I was able to accomplish a life dream of mine just a year after our break-up.

Shortly after achieving that life dream, I began studying to become a counselor. This was a calling that I had felt for a long time. Due to various factors, I would have had to delay these things for at least some time in our marriage. I may never have picked them up again. Only God knows. At the time, it was difficult to understand why I felt so unsettled about the relationship. *Why would God ask me to let go of a great man who seemed to truly love me?* To my human eyes, it didn't make sense on the surface. Though going through that break-up was painful for both of us, now I understand it as God's way of redirecting our lives to the paths He had in mind for each of us. Going into a marriage without peace would have been disastrous. What wife can serve her husband well if she doesn't feel settled about being married to him? What husband would want to stay in a marriage that he never truly felt right about getting into? Sometimes a break-up turns out to be one of the best things that could happen for you.

Another aspect of your life that is protected through singleness can be time. Time is a precious gift. Dating people you are not called to be with can take a lot of time from other endeavors. It can distract you from living your God-given purpose in that season. It can be a time-waster! In fact, being with the wrong person could even delay getting with your actual spouse. Ask for God's protection over your time. Trust that His timing is protection and seeks the best outcome for our lives.

Waiting is, undoubtedly, one of the most frustrating parts of life. If we learn to approach it from a divine perspective, it could transform our lives. Your Creator loves you so much, even more than you could ever comprehend! He wants to give you a joyful marriage, with the person that He has in mind for you. No marriage will come without trials. Yet, rushing into something that is not ordained by God brings a great risk. God knows what He is doing when He places two people together in marriage. Don't try to put yourself into a marriage that was never ordained by the Author of Love.

CHAPTER 9

Obedience and Trust

W hen God says no, listen. It's easier said than done, isn't it? Obedience is not easy to learn. Truly, we are *children* of God! We want to know *why*—like children. Obeying without knowing why is a challenge for many. Honestly, it's likely a challenge for all but the holiest Christian! We must trust that everything that the Lord asks of us is for our good—even when it does not make sense to our human understanding.

> *"Trust in the LORD with all your heart and lean not on your own understanding; in all your ways submit to Him, and He will make your paths straight."*
> *(Proverbs 3:5-6)*

My Personal Lesson

I have had to learn difficult lessons about obedience in the area of relationships. I pray that sharing my experience will help to shield you from heartache or further heartaches. I have tried online dating several times. I met some amazing and interesting people that way. However, I also had some incredibly dreadful experiences. At a certain point, I realized that meeting people online was stressful for me, especially because I consistently connected with people who lived far away. I realized my strong preference for meeting people in person. Yet over and over, I tried different websites and opened myself up to experiences which proved to be very frustrating. One experience, in particular, stands out. This experience was the catalyst for me to *finally* obey and stay away from online dating. It revealed to me that it was high time to put my search for a spouse into God's hands, instead of taking the search into my own. For a short time, I was "talking" consistently with a man I met online. Let's call him "E." E. possessed many positive qualities, and in some ways, even seemed too good to be true. When we met in person, certain character traits came to light. Once again, the Holy Spirit was illuminating what I needed to know in order to make the decision to not proceed with the relationship. Again, when I prayed and discerned, the answer was "no." My family and friends, from the information they knew, were also not thrilled about E. I knew strongly after our meeting that E. and I were not going to work out.

Having heard "no" from the Holy Spirit, and not feeling peace and joy about proceeding with the relationship, I broke things off. This was only about a month after we initially "met" online. E. showed me his true colors as I attempted to tell him my side. He twisted my words against me and called me names. This man, who professed to be a follower of Christ, used Christ against me. I know now that he was projecting past hurts and unhealed wounds onto me. I counted myself fortunate for getting out of that situation quickly. I was also thankful that we did not live in the same city! Looking back, I can also see the signs of manipulation and a controlling personality.

I'm going to let you in on a little secret: I should never have joined that dating site in the first place. From past experiences, I knew how frustrating online dating was to me. Online dating didn't jive well with me and the way that I prefer to meet and interact with people. It was my own impatience that led me to join the site. Shortly before I joined the site, I had even sensed God leading me to focus on my relationship with Him and not to worry about finding a relationship with a man! In the beginning, a technical glitch kept me from being able to view that man's messages. Now I believe that "technical glitch" was actually God trying to protect me! God wanted to protect me from the entire situation, but I stubbornly went my own way. The situation ended in shattered pieces. *I know that without God's protection, it could have ended much worse.*

God had asked me not to do online dating anymore. I knew that, but I disobeyed. This relationship was the rotten fruit of my disobedience. No person can do anything to deserve any kind of abuse. Yet, through obedience, we can be spared from some unnecessary sufferings. Had I listened to God and stopped before creating a profile on that website, I would have been spared some unnecessary heartbreak. Please, note that I don't believe that *everyone* is called to forsake online dating. God has brought numerous couples together in this way. It is all about seeking God about what He has for you specifically, and following that call.

Through this and other experiences, I have learned the virtue of obedience. I've seen with my own eyes that disobedience only brings pain, just as it did in the very beginning in Eden. Obedience brings blessings, though the blessings may come further down the road. The fruits of our obedience become woven into the tapestry of our lives. Sometimes, the fruits will not be evident during this lifetime. Yet, there are many instances when we will see the payoffs of our obedience.

We, in our limited human minds, truly don't know best. We must cling to faith and realize that our all-knowing, omnipotent Creator knows what He is doing. Learn the voice of the Good Shepherd in your life. Then obey Him, even when you don't understand. He is working for your good and sees the entire picture of what lies up ahead.

> *"And we know that in all things God works for the good of those who love Him, who have been called according to His purpose."*
> *(Romans 8:28)*

CHAPTER 10

Renouncing Fear

D o you have any concerns about aspects of your life that you believe make you less desirable to a potential spouse? These concerns can be numerous. They are often related to health problems, familial conflicts, having a child (or children), past mistakes, poverty, etc. The list goes on. There could also be fears related to divorce, abuse, and history repeating in other undesirable ways. A friend confided that he worries about messing a marriage up and letting his future wife down. Insert your own fear(s) here. Fear is a big ol' lie. *No person who has gotten married came from a perfect life. No married person has ever been perfect!* Fear keeps us from hoping for or receiving the blessings God has in store for us.

Letting Go of Fear

No matter if your fears are related to marriage or not, fear keeps you from living in freedom. Christ loved you enough to *die* for you! Don't you think it's possible to meet a human being who will be overjoyed to marry you? Maybe your spouse even has the same "issue." These "issues" can often be reframed as strengths in our lives. It is through suffering that we are refined and become stronger people. We can allow these hardships and challenges in our lives to grow us closer to God. These issues can become the battlefield on which we fight for the true version of ourselves, which will eventually bless our future families and the generations after!

Our "issues" are often things that are possible to work on. Some of the things we fear that will keep us from marriage are areas in which the situation can be improved. Many of these are things that God desires to heal in our lives and that of our families. Relying on God's grace, we must continually be seeking to be the best version of ourselves. Some of the "quirks" that you detest about yourself may be endearing and adorable to the one who chooses you. *It's important to remember that the person right for you will be able to accept what you fear will keep someone from loving you.*

Give your fears to God. The person for you will accept the issues that you are so concerned about. The right person will love you in spite of them. If your "issue" is a sin that needs to be addressed, they will be able to have compassion and meet you where you are. They'll want to fight with you for the good. There is a poignant moment in the film, *Slumdog Millionaire*, when the man that Latika has tried to run from, but has loved her for so long, kisses her scar. The scar and how it came to be is a part of her story. He loves her for it. **Your story is part of who you are.** All the experiences in your life have added up to make up *you*! Over anyone else, your future spouse will choose you! Don't let your fears put limitations on you or your dreams of who you will marry!

Some of the beauty of marriage is vulnerability. Vulnerability is beautiful and terrifying at the same time. Some of us even fear vulnerability itself. Marriage brings the opportunity to continually uncover new layers of the one whom you chose to love for a lifetime. Frequently, even new layers of ourselves are revealed. Some of those layers may be new to us, and many will be new to our spouse as we go through life together. The pressures of life allow these vulnerabilities to be further exposed. Whether you like it or not, your spouse will see you at your good, bad, and very repulsive moments. Learn to be vulnerable with God and others. This will ease the transition into vulnerability with your spouse. Vulnerability with safe people is a rewarding and relationship-building experience.

I can't finish out this chapter without writing about the fear of being alone. Many singles struggle with this at some point, or continually. Remember that being alone is *much* better than being in a destructive or stagnant relationship. Remember also that you are never actually alone. There are people around you. You have a guardian angel. Your Creator is also always with you, whether you can feel His presence or not. If you truly do feel alone, why is that? Pray into it. Do you need to find a better community? Are you actually isolating yourself, and the feeling of aloneness is becoming a self-fulfilling prophecy? Do you have wounds from your childhood (or another part of your life) that need to be addressed? I also recommend solid Christian counseling if you continually struggle with fears of being alone or feelings of loneliness.

Friends, our God is bigger than any fear you have! When you truly desire to let go of fear and walk boldly out of your comfort zone, ask Him for help. He will be with you to break every fear which holds you back from living an abundant life in Him!

Dear Jesus,

You went to the cross and gave it all for me. I pray in Your holy name, Jesus, against the fear of (insert specific fears). I renounce fear and I rebuke it right now, in the name of Jesus! I pray for a renewed and cleansed mind. I pray for a spirit of sound mind and a spirit of boldness. I praise and thank You, Jesus, for delivering me from all my fears!

Amen.

CHAPTER 11

A Time for Healing

A long season of singleness is a perfect opportunity for healing. It is a time to strive towards wholeness. This time is actually a great gift to be thankful for. Too many people have entered into marriage not realizing the extent of their baggage from the past, or how their past will impact their marriage. Some have the situation of working out their baggage in marriage—others divorce when the heaviness of this baggage on the marriage becomes apparent.

For reasons that might only be known to God right now, you are still single. This means that you have the time and space to find healing and walk into marriage a more healed person. This is the time for healing and walking confidently into the future. **The process will stretch you beyond imagining, but it will lead to blessings.**

Steps to Wholeness

We are all broken somehow. We've all endured disappointments and pain. None of us on this earth is without sin. All of us will still be "in-process" until the day we die. Life is an ongoing journey. Yet, when one has actively undergone a healing process, it enables one to become more self-aware. You will know the areas of hurt within your life and be able to be more proactive about addressing them. When new areas of awareness surface in your life, you'll also know how to handle them in a constructive manner.

When both people in a couple are working to become the best version of themselves, their relationship will have an advantage over those who are content to stay the way they are. Those who are not aware of the areas in their lives needing change inevitably hurt others. They even hurt themselves because they are blinded to the ways that they are stuck. Your spouse will be so blessed to marry you, a person firm in your identity in Christ and on your healing journey! I pray that each of you will have begun this healing journey prior to marriage.

A Path to Healing

What are the steps to healing and wholeness? *No person's healing journey will look exactly the same.* Each person has different wounds. God works in unique ways in the life of each individual. Healing isn't a linear journey, either. As you grow into a closer relationship with God and greater awareness of yourself, you'll be able to see the special ways that God is working on your behalf. The steps outlined below are ones that I personally have taken advantage of, as well as known others who took these steps and found deep healing within their lives.

1. **Come to know the Trinity.** I don't mean you should come to know *about* the Trinity; I mean to *really* know the Trinity in a deep and up-close way! God wants a personal relationship with every one of us. Each Person of the Trinity has taught and healed me in a specific way. My Heavenly Father has given me security and knowledge of who I am in Him. Jesus Christ, Savior of us all, walked with me through brokenness into resurrections in my life. The Holy Spirit teaches, guides, and gives me a vision for life. When you come to know the One Who is over all and in Whom all things hold together, you will never be the same! Don't just rely on what others have told you or what you've heard at church. Carve out intentional time daily for God. Don't just talk during your prayer time; also make sure to *listen* to what God has to speak to you! Learn the voice of God in your life.

Study the Holy Scriptures. Soak in them. I know that the Bible can be a struggle for some people to understand. I'd recommend a Bible study, which can help it make more sense and bring the Scriptures to life. The Bible is so rich with connections between the Old and New Testaments! Though we are many years past when the Bible was written, it is definitely still relevant and applicable to our lives today. Ask the Holy Spirit to enlighten you each time that you read the Bible. Learn about Lectio Divina.[6] This way of praying with the Bible and "hearing" God speak to you has been a part of the Christian tradition for hundreds of years. Scripture is nourishment on our journey.

2. **Seek out healing prayer.** In my own journey, I found that being prayed over was a huge step in my healing process. The Holy Spirit brought much healing and awareness to me through healing prayer. I came to encounter the love and healing touch of Jesus Christ. Words of knowledge were also given to me, which helped me to steer onto my life's path and into God's good plans for me. These words of knowledge also helped me to understand in a deeper way what was going on within me and in the spiritual realm of my life. My life and my understanding of my path would be very

---

[6] https://www.contemplativeoutreach.org/what-lectio-divina

different had I not heard the voice of the Holy Spirit through these words of knowledge.

Perhaps your church offers prayer teams, and you can take advantage of healing prayer. If your church does not have this wonderful resource, search and ask around for reputable prayer groups or prayer teams.[7]

3. **Forgive.** Forgiveness is crucial to healing. There might be another person or people you need to forgive. The person you need to forgive could even be yourself! There are those who may even need to let go of anger and resentment towards God. Unforgiveness is like carrying around a heavy bag filled with garbage and weights. It prevents you from receiving God's love fully. Often, it is a barrier to healing. It also prevents you from loving others and spreading the love of God throughout the earth. Jesus gave us the perfect example of forgiveness when He took upon the punishment for the sins of every single person who ever existed. Jesus suffered and died for every single one of us! He even died for the person who hurt you the worst. Cry out to Jesus Christ when you have difficulty forgiving. Speak with a pastor or a counselor if you feel led to do so.

---

[7] You could also search for prayer teams in your area which use the "Unbound" method.

4. **Try counseling.** Throw away your misconceptions about therapy being for crazy people. I am very pro-counseling. I might be a bit biased since I have a degree in counseling, but hear me out! Many individuals and families have made huge strides alongside a competent therapist. Therapy gives you an outside viewpoint, someone to help you explore what is going on inside of you and how the past still affects you. They can also work with you to gain awareness about how exterior circumstances are affecting you, and help you strategize how to commit to positive life changes. I recommend a counselor with a Christian worldview. A counselor with a secular worldview may find it difficult to understand your values, and some may want you to try techniques or buy into ideas that are opposed to Christian beliefs. Meeting with a counselor who has the same understanding of life and eternity is, in my opinion, the preferable option.

5. **Find a supportive community.** We all need a family. Feeling as if you are alone is one of the most difficult and empty feelings we can endure. Even though we may feel alone, the reality is that we are not. Of course, blood family can be a great support for some. For others, their familial relationships bring stress and more pressure to

get married. Many of my other single friends and I have found that being surrounded by friends on the same journey becomes its own type of family. I have other "sisters" that I am walking through extended singleness with. They are honestly one of the biggest blessings in my life. When I talk to them about my experiences and feelings, *they get it*. It's difficult to walk through these situations without people who understand, so make sure that some of your friends do "get it." Married couples are also a part of my community. Some of them waited for God's best until their 30's, even close to 40, and are now in joyful marriages. Each unique relationship weaves strands of beauty and wisdom into my life.

Being a member of a supportive, growth-oriented church is also an aspect of community. Find a church where you can get involved. You need people who love you for who you are but also encourage you to grow deeper into your identity as a daughter or son of God. A strong community stirs you to become the best version of yourself. It's essential to walk alongside people who inspire you and are also seeking wholeness. It's amazing to witness the person you become and how your perception of yourself changes based upon the circles you are surrounding yourself with. A positive circle can change everything! People who bring you down only hurt you and hold you back from being the best version of yourself.

6. **Take care of yourself holistically.** There are many facets to human beings. We are more than simply a body walking around. Each facet of our self affects the other facets. What does being a holistic, integrated person include? It means taking care of your body and feeding it the foods it needs to function well. The foods you eat can even affect your moods and how you are thinking and feeling mentally. Your body also needs exercise, which can help stave off depression or decrease depressive symptoms. Sleep is another crucial aspect of our health. Lack of sleep magnifies problems and lessens our ability to think clearly about them. Fatigue distorts our thinking and our moods. This, in turn, can negatively affect our relationships with others.

Caring for and nurturing your mental health is vastly important. Surround yourself with positivity. It's amazing the extent to which being around people who degrade you can negatively affect your perception of yourself. Also, be mindful about your media intake. These things do affect us, especially over time. Embrace being in the classroom of life. Read books about new topics or topics that interest you.

Stimulate your mind. This will open up new avenues for your life, and make you more interesting to potentials and the person who is, well, "the one!" As I mentioned before, eating nutritious foods can also go a long way in keeping your mind functioning well.

One aspect of mental health is acknowledging our emotions. Emotions send us important messages about our true mental state and our lives. Trying to ignore emotions isn't productive, as they often worsen and show up in other ways. When something seemingly small upsets us, that's a trigger. That trigger can let you know about areas within you which Jesus longs to fully heal. Praying about these things can be helpful, as the Holy Spirit will help you to be aware of the root. Getting healing prayer is also a great idea.

Cultivating healthy thought processes is essential to mental health. Look for critical thoughts about yourself and others. Watch for limiting and negative thought processes. Of course, I'm also going to mention solid Christian counseling once again if you're interested in getting insight into some of these areas!

I am not going to neglect mentioning the most vital aspect of you—your soul! I've mentioned prayer countless times throughout this book—because it's crucial! Put simply, it's a conversation with God. In your prayer time, you can be completely honest with God! There's nothing to hide from

Him. A relationship with God builds a firm foundation for our lives. If you don't have a solid prayer life, start to build that foundation now! It's something so easy to keep putting off. If not now, then when will you start? Satan takes great pleasure in distracting us from prayer. At first, prayer may not be easy. It's hard for some personality types to be still and have quiet time. There are many ways to pray, and different personalities have certain ways that they may prefer to pray. Figure out how you best connect to God. Set aside that time for God as if it's the most important part of your day. Then, pray and watch as your life, the lives of your future family, and the people around you, are transformed due to your bold and patient intercession!

You Are Enough

There can be the temptation to believe that you are incomplete because you are without a "special" person in your life. The world can make a person feel like that. Sadly, even the Church (or her members) fosters this belief sometimes. You can make yourself feel as if you're not enough, watching as it seems that everyone but you is pairing up and growing a family. As the questions and shocked looks come from others due to your single state, it's not difficult to start questioning if something is wrong. Is there some defect on your part? Isn't it better to be paired up? What can be done to speed up the process? **Stop!**

"For You created my inmost being;
You knit me together in my mother's
womb. I praise You because I am
fearfully and wonderfully made;
Your works are wonderful, I know
that full well."
(Psalm 139:13-14)

This chapter was written as I prepared to get my picture taken for the church directory. Yes, I will be the only person present in the picture. I won't even have a pet to be with me in the picture. But I'm going to dress up and shine! *I am beautiful, and I am of value.* I am a complete person. I do not need another person to complete me. I am made in the image of God, fearfully and wonderfully made. *So are you.* Take the time and steps you need in order to heal. Your future self, future spouse, and future children will thank you. Remember that you are loved and accepted by the greatest Love, no matter what! The place you are in now is not the place you will stay, as long as you rely on God's grace and believe that your life can change and you can walk into greater wholeness.

CHAPTER 12

The Gifts of Wisdom & Clarity

*T*he Bible talks a lot about wisdom. We all need wisdom in order to live lives of righteousness and to follow God's path for us. Being single longer than expected has provided me ample time to gain wisdom. I am not speaking only of general wisdom, though there's been plenty of time for that, too. I am talking now about the wisdom to discern my marriage partner.

> *"How much better to get wisdom*
> *than gold,*
> *to get insight rather than silver!"*
> *(Proverbs 16:16)*

Clarity Changes Choices

Have you ever come to realize that the person (or type of person) you would have chosen to marry a few years ago is very different than the person you would choose today? I think that many people who find themselves single later than expected have this experience. In my early twenties, I would have definitely had a different choice in a marriage partner. I am so thankful that God graced me with different life experiences and provided this time of clarity. As a younger lady, it's not something I knew I needed. Thankfully, God certainly knew!

In the school of life, I have learned many valuable lessons. Now, I can confidently say that I know much better regarding what to look for in a potential husband and potential father of my children. Through my experiences, dating and otherwise, the Holy Spirit has been clear about what to look for. I am more discerning about whom I date or even consider dating. Some people are secure in who they are and choose a suitable marriage partner at a young age. Even those people whose identity was secure at a younger age may still need to wait longer for a spouse. Those like me simply had another path to walk out, one which brought greater clarity about their lives and futures.

Being single for an extended time has its share of difficulties. Yet, there are also benefits to this time. Here are some of the main ways that I believe a person can gain wisdom from extended singleness. I, and other single people I know, have experienced many of these things.

1. **You are able to observe many relationships & marriages.** This can give you a vantage point to determine the qualities you hope for in a partner. You will be able to pinpoint what you desire in a marriage, and what you definitely do not want. In some small way, you can see the good, the bad, the struggles, and the ugly as other relationships play out. Your observation of different relationships and talking to those you know who are courting, engaged, or married will give you wisdom. You have the advantage of learning from the successes, challenges, and even the mistakes of others.

2. **Longer singlehood gives you time to gain clarity.** Marrying young can turn out to be detrimental for some, as they have not yet realized a specific direction in their lives. They may not have had the time and experiences to clarify their purpose that those who are single for a longer period of time have. A person who waits longer for marriage is generally more mature and has had more life experiences to gain clarity about what direction their life is headed. A longer time of singleness (and past

relationships) can also provide clarity about what you are and are not looking for in a marriage partner.

3. **Finding life in Jesus Christ is what brings true joy.** Living a longer time of singleness can also reveal that marriage is not the "be all, end all" of life. Some may have carried that attitude as younger singles. As you embrace the gifts present within life, you realize Who gave you those gifts. Over time, you gain a greater appreciation for each gift, even if it's not the one that you prayed for. As life unfolds, it becomes clear that our expectations of life and the Heavenly Father's plan are often different. This can lead us closer to God as we lean on Him for answers to our questions! As you turn more and more to Christ and see His faithfulness revealed, you see that He is truly what satisfies in life.

Wisdom and Clarity Are Teachers

The clarity that you discover as a single person can bless your marriage, future family, and maybe even a ministry as husband and wife. As you grow older, your vision becomes wider. You are more aware of the direction your life is headed. My time of singleness has clarified the purpose that God created me for. There are some very specific callings in my life. Over time, these have become strikingly clear. *I cannot marry just anyone.* The man that I marry will need to understand and have a similar calling in his life. If we are not united in our goals and vision, we will be going in different directions. Had I married younger, I would not have known these things about myself. I did not have the healing or vision back then that I have now. Marriage could have been a disaster. I am grateful now that I have a clearer vision for moving forward into marriage and family life. That clarity and vision are very freeing. I am easily able to recognize when something or someone does not fit into that vision. When I see someone who does fit into that vision, it's also easy to spot that.

We can also obtain wisdom that is applicable to our specific personalities. The Lord allows the circumstances of our lives that will refine and purify us in the specific way needed. A parent disciplines their child so the child will learn what they need to learn. It's similar to our Heavenly Father. One of the virtues I struggle with the most is patience. So, guess what? I have waited longer for everything in my life. I waited longer for my first car, for my first apartment, for my first professional job, and the list goes on! Case in point: I am past age 30, and I'm still awaiting the time of knowing my dear husband and starting a family! Obviously, patience is one lesson that I needed to learn. It's something I'm still learning every day.

What is it that the Lord is highlighting for you through your period of singleness? If it is not clear to you, ask your Creator what He intends to teach you through the experiences of your life. In our difficulties, there is always something we can learn. He will make it clearer to you when you ask Him. However, please don't fall into believing the lie that being single is a punishment. It is not. While it can be very refining, our God isn't about keeping people single because of past mistakes or beliefs about themselves. He has many good gifts to give you. It just may be that it is not your time to be married yet. Or, He may have a gift other than marriage to give you.

Clarity Frees Us

Now, I have no regrets about realizing someone is not for me. It's important to discern and have a heart of openness. But I also realize that there are people who just aren't for me. It's the same for you. That's okay. There is no need to force something which wasn't meant to be. We don't need to waste our time or theirs. There are certain qualities that I am set on for my husband and the father of my children. I now also ask myself how a man will fit into the greater vision God has revealed for my life. More importantly, I pray about it! As a younger person, I really didn't have a clue. I thought you simply married someone because you loved them. Marrying someone due to shared vision and purpose wasn't yet as salient in my thought processes. Now, my Heavenly Father has laid out a clearer path. It's important to know what you're looking for in a spouse, so that you can recognize it (or them) when it is in front of you. Keep character traits at the forefront of your mind so that you can recognize a virtuous person.

There is another aspect to clarity, and that is knowing *what* and *who* we are responsible for in this life. It is very necessary to realize that we cannot change someone. Say you are dating someone with numerous great qualities. However, there is one big aspect of their character or detail about their life that bothers you. You decide to go forward with engagement and marriage, believing that you can change that aspect of them. First of all, no one can change a person except God. A person needs an open heart in order for that work to be done. You can have an *influence* on another person, but it is not the same as changing them. Next, whatever bothers you before marriage will still bother you after you marry them. In fact, it will probably bother you ten times worse than before you were married. I'm not speaking as a married person, but I've heard it from many married people. The more you are around someone, the more you notice things and see whatever it is that bothers you. Pay attention to how malleable a person is, and how open they are to working on their character.

Peace and Clarity

Pay attention when you don't have peace. Peace is a big sign that moving forward is a positive thing. *Lack of peace needs to be paid attention to.* If the peace isn't there, pray about why this is so. If the situation can be changed, discuss it with the person. Don't continue if peace eludes you despite prayer, counsel, and other efforts. If you're seeing or talking to someone and the peace still isn't there, dragging it out won't change anything. It's going to end up hurting the other person, and probably both of you, in the end. If it isn't meant to be, no amount of praying, talking it out with the person, or asking for advice, is going to bring you peace. I've definitely been in situations where I realized, deep down, that it wasn't right. But I continued to ask for advice, thinking that it might change the situation or the way I felt. It didn't.

Peace comes from the Holy Spirit. A sure sign of a right relationship is an overwhelming sense of peace. I'm not talking about the peace which comes after you rationalize to yourself (or others) the red flags and aspects of a person's life that you really wish weren't present. I'm talking about true peace which surpasses understanding. There's nothing we can do to gain that peace. It's something that God will grant to us when it is right.

When you meet a "person of interest," ask the Holy Spirit to reveal to you what you need to see. Believe me: this prayer will be answered, and usually quite quickly! While each of my experiences so far has shown what I need to see to make sure that the relationship doesn't continue—I look forward to the day when the Holy Spirit continually reveals the beauty and the rightness of that person for me, and the rightness of me for him!

I believe that the clarity God has given me about His plan for my life is a great gift. I know many other singles who have found this clarified purpose during their extended singleness. I also have a sense that some of you reading will find more clarity by meeting your spouse. For some of you reading, God will reveal a new purpose as you and your spouse journey together. For all of us, the Holy Spirit will continue to lead us in our lives as we surrender.

Desire to be a person of wisdom. Seek out wisdom by surrounding yourself with wise and righteous people. If you feel that you lack clarity about your life's direction and even whether or not you'll be married one day, seek God's heart on the matter. Ask the Holy Spirit for clarity and wisdom. Study Sacred Scripture. Clarity is a gift, and it brings a new sense of peace and freedom to life. If clarity is something that you feel is still lacking in your life, I pray that the Lord grants you this priceless gift.

"But the Advocate, the Holy Spirit, whom the Father will send in My name, will teach you all things and will remind you of everything I have said to you." (John 14:26)

CHAPTER 13

Openness

*P*erhaps it seems silly that I'm writing a chapter on openness directly after a chapter on clarity. Yet, it is very necessary for me to do so. Clarity is important because it allows you not to waste your time or another person's time. Clarity enables you to focus on living out God's call for you. It empowers you not to waste time wondering about or trying out relationships that are clearly not suitable for you. However, there is also a need for a dose of openness as we search for our spouses. Open your ears and your heart as you read this chapter. I know that I'm primarily speaking to my sisters in this chapter. However, brothers, listen up. I know that men aren't immune to the matters that I'm going to cover in this chapter.

Superhuman Fantasies

A single sister of mine and I spoke about a phenomenon that has happened during our years of being single—the years between when we expected to be wed and the year that is now, years later (when we remain unwed). We have had time to create, in our minds, the superhero of a man that will be our husband. He'll be fine, of course, but also have very refined character. His weaknesses will be difficult to discern because he is just so *holy*. He ministers to others and is perhaps is even well known. It is very likely he even started his ministry himself. We'll meet, and we're going to be the ministry partner that he's always dreamed about. Together, we're going to minister and bring droves of people to Christ.

Stop the fantasies. Some of these may be true, but you don't know *exactly* the story that God is writing. You are going to marry a flesh and blood human being. Like you, he (or she) has areas of weakness to struggle through. Perhaps you are even the person that God has chosen to bring healing to him (or her). He may be (and very likely is) a person that God has chosen to bring healing to you in some way. Yes, he or she will be attractive to you (though at times, physical attraction may not come until later on in your relationship). I've heard from many married people, though, that their spouse actually ended up not being their "type!" It is also possible that you will be called to a specific ministry together. All married couples are called to evidently demonstrate the love of Christ and His Church to the world. However, we need to let go of our fantasies and allow Christ to work out the *reality*. When a characteristic about the person or their life doesn't match our fantasy, we'll end up disappointed. *No one wants their greatness to be overlooked because of a person who doesn't actually exist.*

Reality Looks Different

Some of you expect a person to act a certain way, look a certain way, and even enter your life in a certain way. *What if your idea is never what God intended?* Some of the best gifts of my life have come from being open. These gifts have come in highly unexpected ways. *We are not ultimately the authors of our stories. God is.* That, my friends, is beautiful. It takes the pressure off us. We don't need to try to take control. **We can simply let God be God!**

Learn to be open to others wherever they are at on their journey. Your husband or wife isn't going to be a "finished product" when you meet them. We are all "in process." Life is not as black and white as we think or wish. We can be too open, however. If there is something glaring about your relationship or the person that tugs at your heart and just won't let you settle down, pay attention. If you feel like you are settling and your heart sinks because you just wish that things were different, *then don't settle*. Don't sacrifice a cheerful heart because you desire to be married and this person seems to be the best option at the time. New doors can open, and your God-chosen spouse can unexpectedly walk through those doors!

In our preferences, we must also have a healthy level of willingness to let go. I believe that the Lord does give us the desires of our hearts. However, the way that He grants them may be different. Your spouse may be a different race or of a different ethnicity than you expected. They may be a little older than you thought they'd be. They may even be *younger* than you hoped for, but surprisingly mature. The person may be taller or shorter than you anticipated. Bring it to prayer. Sometimes, the best gifts in life are a surprise!

Men, please be patient with women. Sometimes, we can be very set in our minds. I apologize for any times that you been overlooked unnecessarily. I apologize for any pride that has kept us from seeing your goodness and your character. Pray that the Holy Spirit will show us what we need to know. We're praying the same for you.

CHAPTER 14

A Suitable Partner

There is a lot of emphasis placed on compatibility nowadays. This is a good thing; don't get me wrong. There is nothing wrong with compatibility. Yet, compatibility by itself is fleeting and on the surface. There are many more ingredients that go into creating a lifelong marriage. What is to be desired more than compatibility? *Suitability.*

Compatibility vs. Suitability

In Genesis 2:18, The LORD God said, *"It is not good for the man to be alone. I will make a helper suitable for him."* There are many people we could be compatible with. "Compatible" is defined as "able to exist or act together harmoniously."[8] Notice that the definition says "able to." There are many things we are "able" to do, but that does not mean that we need to do all of them. "Able" also brings to mind the idea of survival, and not of thriving. I want to look beyond being "able to" do something and know that there is something greater or higher. There are many jobs we are "able" to do, but many are below our highest abilities. There are also fewer people that we are suitable to and for than those that we could be compatible with. "Suitable" is defined as "right or appropriate for a particular person, purpose, or situation."[9] To me, suitability speaks of the *best possible fit.* With compatibility, there are positives. Yet, there may be missing puzzle pieces or pieces that don't quite fit. With suitability, on the other hand, the puzzle is complete. Suitability takes everything into account: a person's calling and life purpose, as well as the other factors that compatibility looks at, such as personality or interests.

The Lord cared so much about Adam that He created a partner suitable for him. It is the same with us. If we wait on Him, He will bring into our lives a person suitable for us. Not just a person that is okay for us. Not simply a person "compatible" with us on the surface. He wants to bring together people who will complement one another. It has

---

[8] The Merriam-Webster dictionary
[9] https://en.oxforddictionaries.com/definition/compatible

been a delight to watch many of my friends marry at older than average ages. As I watch them meet, court, and marry their spouses, it has been so clear why they were asked to wait. The world may have viewed their marriages as being "late." However, it was actually God's perfect timing for them. Through all their trials, breakups, and life experiences, God was preparing them for the marriage He had in mind all along. God is truly the best Matchmaker!

I had numerous experiences living with different roommates. But then, I had one where it just "clicked." Our personalities were very similar, and we lived together peacefully as if we had known each other all of our lives. The experience was smooth and blessed. Even the way we met was clearly divinely orchestrated. I will never forget that season where we lived together. I look back on it and miss it. Going home truly was like *going home*. I think that experience of "clicking" and the rightness and peace of the situation is a taste of what it will be like to meet my husband. I believe that if I wait on the man that God has for me (however long that wait may turn out to be), it will be similar to that roommate experience. To be clear, I do realize that there will be adjustments as a man learns to live with me, and I learn to live with him! Relationships with people take communication, time, and learning to understand one another. Yet I do believe that the suitable partners who we are waiting upon will complement us and balance us out, bringing elements to our lives which we will greatly benefit from. There is a sense of comfort and safety with a suitable partner.

I think of past relationships with men where something just didn't seem quite right. We may have been compatible in various ways, but we were not *suitable* for one another. We could talk and laugh easily. We enjoyed the same or similar hobbies. We could sing along to the same music. Yet, when it came to similar life goals or values in certain areas, that suitability just wasn't there. I tried to bring up certain dreams for the future, but they couldn't understand these dreams. Our lives were clearly going in different directions. We were not suitable for one another. Marriage would have been difficult due to those "missing pieces."

When it comes to the person you will marry, peace should be present when you are in the presence of that person. There should be security. You shouldn't need to feel that you have to hide anything from that person. You should feel the freedom to act in a genuine way and to express your feelings. You should be free to be open and vulnerable and share anything. With the right person, there will not be a need to hide any part of you or make any part of you lesser in order to make that person stay. That is a fear-based relationship, not based on love. Pay attention when something doesn't feel quite right in your relationship with a person, then figure out what's going on. Pay close attention when it does feel right and figure out what promotes the rightness of the relationship. Over time, you'll see patterns in the different relationships in your life and discover the types of people that you are most suitable for. Don't discount compatibility. But please, focus on *suitability*.

CHAPTER 15

The Chapter on Chastity

*Y*es, I am going to devote this entire chapter to chastity. Our sex drive is something we deal with on a daily basis, so let's talk about it. I know it's somewhat ironic that I'm writing this chapter. Earlier in the book, I wrote of my annoyance about the numerous purity talks I attended, which did not teach me about other important aspects of a relationship. However, chastity is a necessary topic. Especially for those who did not expect to be living abstinence (or struggling to abstain) for so long, it is a daily issue. This can be a difficult topic. By God's grace, I'm going to delve into it. I pray that I can give it some sort of justice. What I promise not to do is stray from the truth!

Before I go any further, I want to note that sexual abuse is a devastation which various men and women around the world have lived through. If this happened to you, I am so sorry. At any stage of life, this is a traumatic occurrence. If this is something which you endured, it was not your fault. Please seek a godly and compassionate counselor who is experienced working with survivors of this type of abuse. Abuse can affect how you relate to your spouse within marriage, and this type of abuse is not an exception to that. Sometimes this type of abuse can even lead to promiscuity, as the person tries to gain a sense of control in this area. Other times, it can lead to difficulty with intimacy. There is always healing with Jesus Christ on our side, no matter how distressing the experiences we have suffered in this life. In this chapter, I am focusing upon what we are in control of.

More Than Physical

Chastity is more than simply refraining from sex. It is a posture of living with our hearts in the right place. It encompasses our thoughts, intentions, our view of others, and our actions. Living a chaste life means living a life of freedom. It definitely doesn't always seem so. According to our Creator's design, married people have rightful access to certain pleasures that single people do not. Yet, just as in the case of all the commandments, this one is also for our good and the good of others.

By living a pure life, you are being faithful to your spouse before you even meet them! In Proverbs 31:12, it says of a wife that **"she does him good and not evil all the days of her life."** Did you notice how the verse said *all* the days of her life? Not just after she meets him. Not just after they get married. She honors him every single day of her life! Men, apply this to yourselves too. There is no double standard; men *and* women are held to a standard of purity. The battle for purity is one that we must fight each day of our lives.

"For our struggle is not against flesh and blood, but against the rulers, against the authorities, against the powers of this dark world and against the spiritual forces of evil in the heavenly realms." (Ephesians 6:12)

Purity deals with our emotions and our thoughts. It's important to be cautious about what entertainment you are taking in. Sometimes, romantic comedies, love songs, and even clean romance novels can weigh on a person's heart and make being single even more difficult. They can lead to fake scripts in our minds. Be careful about the thought processes and the thoughts that you let play in your mind. Women especially tend to create fantasies in their minds. A meeting and a first date go amazingly well, and we find ourselves starstruck by the man in question. We tell our closest gal friends, and before we know it, we're planning the wedding and thinking about how well our first name pairs with his last name. All this is even before a conversation about the future has taken place between the man and you! Down the road, these emotional attachments are going to hurt. Also, when we feel lonely, it's easy to form emotional attachments. I firmly believe that we must *let go* of these people and our attachments to them before God will bring our spouses into our lives, or before we can recognize our spouses. Even forming an emotional attachment too quickly to the person that will be your spouse could be potentially unhealthy. Pacing a relationship and setting boundaries is essential.

Avoid emotional flings with people you know are not the ones that the Lord has for you. Yes, being single for a long time can be lonely. It doesn't need to equate to looking for emotional validation from the wrong person or people. Do you have a healthy community around you who is providing affirmation? Seek to be around these people. Yet if you continually find yourself searching for validation from others, it's time to do some deep soul searching and conversing with your Heavenly Father.

Purity Has Benefits

Finding a spouse is complicated enough without adding sex to the mix! If you're messing around or having sex, it could be delaying you from meeting your spouse. It's taking time away from building a relationship with God. Having sex outside of marriage is actually lying to yourself and sinning against your own body, as we learn in Scripture. Fornicating is building soul ties with someone that is (possibly) not meant to be your spouse. Even if you are seriously dating (or even engaged to) that person, it does not mean that you will marry them. Having sex takes time away from focusing on issues that are important to concentrate upon together before committing to a lifetime with another person. Sexual pleasure can blind you to red flags and other matters that need to be dealt with before marriage.

There are so many benefits to living chastely, even beyond knowing that you are following God's law. Chastity frees you from premature responsibility.[10] Purity brings emotional freedom, as you are not building emotional attachments to someone who is not meant to be your spouse. It also frees you from the awkwardness that can occur after sharing intimate parts of yourself with someone else before

---

[10] Babies are always blessings, but it's also a blessing for a child to be born into a healthy marriage.

the God-ordained time. During sexual activity, oxytocin is released. This is a bonding hormone. During marriage, this hormone is beneficial and helps to boost your relationship and strengthen your bond even in difficult times.[11]

"Flee from sexual immorality. All other sins a person commits are outside the body, but whoever sins sexually, sins against their own body."
(1 Corinthians 6:18)

Be Practical

There are some practical tips that can be used to help fight this battle. Avoid people, places, and things that are tempting. That might mean changing up the TV shows and movies you're watching, the music you're listening to, and what you are reading. Regular exercise is also helpful for many of those trying to be chaste. Be wise about spending time with the opposite sex alone. Making common sense choices, such as not laying down together and going your separate ways after a certain hour, can go a long way in

---

[11]https://neuro.hms.harvard.edu/harvard-mahoney-neuroscience-institute/brain-newsletter/and-brain/love-and-brain

helping you stay strong. Setting clear boundaries from the beginning of a relationship is crucial. As you get closer to someone, the temptation is likely to increase. Daily time for reading the Scriptures and praying is greatly important to keep yourself rooted in the greatest relationship of your life.

Once a person has been sexually active or tasted some type of sexual intimacy with another person, those actions aren't difficult to initiate again. With chastity, a person must make the *absolute decision* that they are going to be pure. Do not leave openings or cracks for "something" to happen. Chastity is something you must strongly desire. If you're a part of a couple, it's so key that both of you are on the same page about this. Staying away from situations that tempted you in the past or that you know would tempt you now is a must. Otherwise, it's much too easy to get caught up in passion again and to leave openings for sin. Having people that you are accountable to is helpful in this regard. Please, make sure they're people that you can be honest with. Oftentimes, people in the Church are not comfortable with this topic. Let's work to change this! It's so important to have friends who are also seeking to live righteously and can be trusted to honestly share your struggles and triumphs with.

Pornography might be a struggle for you. In order to break free, it's crucial to find accountability. That might mean putting a special filter on your devices or having people around you who are committed to helping you break free. Preferably, it would be both. There are even apps that are committed to providing support and help during your time of breaking free.[12] Pornography is a scourge that is widespread even in the Church. Porn destroys marriages and even affects relationships before they start. Porn leads to a distorted sense of reality and expectations which no real person can meet. Being aware of your struggle and being willing to get help now will have great fruits for your life and future marriage. You aren't the first person to fight an addiction, and you also won't be the last one to overcome one, by the grace of God!

"No temptation has overtaken you except what is common to mankind. And God is faithful; He will not let you be tempted beyond what you can bear. But when you are tempted, He will also provide a way out so that you can endure it." (1 Corinthians 10:13)

---

[12] Check out the free "Victory" app in the Google Play Store.

Chastity Brings Freedom

Chastity is empowering. Living chastely allows us to live in the freedom that is our inheritance as the royal children of God. It helps us not to base our worth on another person's value of us, but to find our security in our identity as a child of God. I know that I'm worthy of a lifetime commitment with a man who loves God above all and is committed to treating me as a daughter of the King. My friend, you are worthy of a spouse who treats you the same: as the son or daughter of the Heavenly Father!

Living lives of chastity also provides us the freedom to live as brothers and sisters. We grow in intimacy with one another—not sexually, but developing in a gradual understanding of who the other person is. We learn to see them as a fellow child of God instead of making them an object for our pleasure. *That, my friend, is a beautiful gift.* One day, perhaps one of these friendships will be awakened into a deeper friendship, one that leads to a life lived together for the rest of your lives. That would be a beautiful revelation, made all the more beautiful for having a pure history together. A friendship lived in chastity and mutual respect builds a glorious foundation for a lifelong marriage. "Friends with benefits" will never bring fulfillment. That isn't a friendship at all, but rather a relationship based on usury. It also dishonors God, yourself, the other person involved, and your future spouse.

'Therefore, I urge you, brothers and sisters, in view of God's mercy, to offer your bodies as a living sacrifice, holy and pleasing to God—this is your true and proper worship."
(Romans 12:1)

This verse has taken on another level of meaning for me as I live out singleness. Celibacy can be a difficult cross. It is truly a call, and not many were intended to live that call for their entire lives. Yet, it is "true and proper worship" of God to sacrifice ourselves! If living in celibacy is how you are called to glorify Him at this very moment, then so be it. This period of celibacy allows you to be more available to serve the Church and the world. Singles lay down the yearnings built into our very bodies, yearnings to share our love in the most intimate way possible with another person and for that love to turn into three. It is a tremendous sacrifice, made even greater by the fact that our desires are completely normal and natural. We are living sacrifices, holy and pleasing to God! Now that's a thought to ponder.

Grace, Mercy, and Forgiveness

No one is perfect. We've all sinned and fallen short of the glory of God. Each of us has areas of our lives that are more difficult for us to live out in a righteous way. Know that God loves you exactly where you are! Repent, confess your sins, and commit to living another way. Really commit—don't leave those openings or even those hopes for opportunities to sin. Commit to changing your relationships, if needed. Again, accountability is a powerful tool. If you've been sexual with someone or some people in the past, it's also important to break any soul ties with them. There are prayers that you can find to do this. You may also enlist a pastor or spiritual leader to help you. Ridding your life of any objects which maintain an unnecessary connection with them is also vital. If you have a child (or children) together, you will still need to work together for the best interests of the child (if it is possible to do so).

It is possible to be pure. It is possible to be abstinent until marriage, even though you may be much older than expected by the time marriage happens. It is possible to start over again if you've fallen in the past. As long as we believe purity is doable and commit wholeheartedly to a chaste way of life, it is an achievable goal. Don't let the world lie to you and say otherwise.

"Create in me a pure heart, O God, and renew a steadfast spirit within me."
(Psalm 51:10)

Dear Heavenly Father,

I commend to you each of those reading this book. I thank You for them and for their desire to follow You. I ask that you cleanse us and purify our hearts. I pray in Jesus' name against any spirit of shame or condemnation. May those spirits of shame and condemnation be replaced instead with the knowledge of the freedom of being children of God. Purify our minds. I pray against the spirit of lust, in the name of Jesus. Replace that spirit with Your Holy Spirit, the Spirit of purity, from head to toe. Give us the supernatural strength to live lives of purity and holiness. Put people alongside us who are committed to the same things and will faithfully walk with us on this journey. I thank and praise You for answering this prayer! In Jesus' name, I pray.

Amen!

CHAPTER 16

The Gift of Time and Seasons

O ur Creator was so intentional in the creation of the world. The earth goes through the same cycles, year after year. Seasons were created for the growth and renewal of the world. Each season serves a specific purpose. No season was created without a clear intention. The winter season allows plants to "rest" and store up energy for new growth. Winter eventually leads to spring and new life. During summer, the sun provides ample energy for life to prosper and continue. Fall is the harvest season, where the fruit of the earlier seasons is born. These seasons mirror our own lives. **You are in the season you are in now for a reason.** Read that again, and let it sink in. This season is somehow preparing you for the future that God planned for you before you were even conceived.

We Have the Present Moment

I spent many hours of my undergraduate days looking out the library window and dreaming of the days of being a wife and mother. I believed that season of my life was just around the corner. Instead of focusing on the task at hand, I looked forward to a future that I romanticized in my mind. I believed that I would find that period of life easier than academic life. (I wonder how my younger self would react if older me could tell her that she'd be past 30 and still be single? Thankfully, life is only revealed little by little.) I spent many hours during my 20's reading articles about relationships, marriage, and parenting. There were even a few baby items that I purchased.

There's nothing wrong with preparing for the future. Preparation reveals faith and readiness. Preparation shows that we're ready to steward what God has for us. However, we need to keep at the forefront of our minds that we don't know about tomorrow. We don't know when our dreams will come to fruition. **All we have for sure is the present moment.**

The fact is, we don't know when the desires of our heart will be fulfilled. Even when our desires are so strong that it feels as if we can't go on without them, it's not our decision when they will manifest. We don't even know how many days on this earth that we'll be gifted with. If you are reading this, you might already know that dreams can be deferred many, many years beyond what you planned.

As I've learned gratitude for the gifts of my current season, contentment has followed. No longer am I so focused on the expected blessings of the future. Each season carries its own blessings. This even includes a seemingly never-ending single season! After the wedding, you're married for life! The married season is one that sticks. Why are we so eager to change seasons? Our Creator has a Divine design for each season of our lives. If fall came early, the fruits of the earth wouldn't be ready for harvest. Let's pray to perceive the beauty and the reason for each of these seasons. Seek to give your best self and full presence to every season of your life.

One vital thing to do during your single season is to learn discipline. As a single person, you have so much time. Perhaps it does not feel like it, but once you have a spouse and children, your time will be split in so many different directions. Ample "free time" becomes a thing of the past. You can focus wholeheartedly now on the Lord and not become distracted. I like to think about the stories I'll tell my children about the places I traveled, the books I wrote, and the types of jobs that I was able to do before they came along. The fact is, I likely would not have had many of these opportunities if I'd married young, as I had planned. This season of singleness, which has stretched long, has planted many seeds and borne fruits. I believe that my future spouse and children and I will be able to together witness the growth of the seeds into strong trees. For those fruits which are already evident, I can't wait to share in them with my future spouse and our children.

Waiting is a Sacred Time

The time of waiting is sacred. God is doing a magnificent work behind the scenes. I think of a seed planted in the ground. On the surface, the seed cannot be seen. It appears that nothing is happening. In reality, intricate things are taking place under the ground. Root systems are growing and becoming secure. After these roots have taken hold, the plant or tree will begin to grow imperceptibly, still underground. Eventually, the plant starts to push above the ground and become visible. It looks like a small sprout, but much more work has taken place than one could even imagine.

Eventually, that tiny sprout becomes much larger. Buds, branches, flowers, and fruit will come forth. Rain, sunshine, and weeding have served different functions in order to ensure the plant's full evolution. All that work has finally become fruitful. Yet for a long time, the work being done could not even be seen! I believe that it's the same with us. In each of our seasons, God is somehow growing and maturing us. It may not be evident on the surface, but when we cooperate with grace, He can make something great out of us. You can become a strong oak of righteousness!

'They will be called oaks of righteousness, a planting of the **LORD** *for the display of His splendor."* *(Isaiah 61:3b)*

God's view of time is drastically different than ours. I like to think that God's view is aerial. He can see every angle, and sees the complete past, the present, and the future. While we are living in the present, it often seems interminable. We need to trust and be assured that God is working powerfully, even when we have no idea what is happening behind the scenes. Even if you are increasing in age, the Lord can play with time. He can drastically change your life in a year. He could send you twins or triplets! Your spouse could bring "bonus babies." You could be led to foster care or adoption, or have neighbor kids whose parents are emotionally absent. There are so many children wounded and seeking an opportunity to be part of a secure, loving family, even if that opportunity only comes after school or for a few hours per week.

I know that for women, the "biological clock" is a struggle. For many women, the desire for motherhood is strong. The good news is that women are often fertile into their 40's! While most people probably envisioned having our children in their 20's and early 30s, we do know that fertility often lasts beyond that. As the world says one thing, we know that God has the final say over our lives and families!

'Things were in God's plan which I had not planned at all. I am coming to the living faith and conviction that—from God's point of view—there is no chance and that the whole of my life, down to every detail, has been mapped out in God's divine providence and makes complete and perfect sense in God's all-seeing eyes.'' St. Edith Stein[13]

There are so many people who squander away the seasons of their lives. For them, the present is a time to pass through while awaiting the next thing. This is a deception. There are people who have wished their lives away. Live with intention, fully present in each season. You are called to serve

---

[13]https://catholic-link.org/quotes/gods-plan-according-st-edith-stein-quote/

and to grow in each season. Life passes by so quickly, even when it seems that a season is going slowly. Savor the season, and discover what you can be grateful for every day.

"But do not forget this one thing, dear friends: With the Lord a day is like a thousand years, and a thousand years are like a day."
(2 Peter 3:8)

CHAPTER 17

A Loving Community

*C*ommunity is a gift that cannot be paralleled. God has provided this gift to me abundantly during my time of singleness. I have numerous single sisters and brothers in my community, so we're all in this together. Were it not for this loving and encouraging community, I am not sure how well I would have survived a long season of singleness. Frankly, I wonder if I would have settled with someone interested, but someone not well-suited to me. Psalm 68:6 tells us that "God sets the lonely in families." Sometimes, that may not yet mean the family of marriage. It may mean a loving church family. It might be wonderful "soul" friends. It may even be a healed relationship, or a closer relationship, with your family of origin.

We Need A Community

Every human being needs a community. Adam was not without human companionship in the Garden for long. God even said in Genesis 2:18 *that it is not good for man to be alone!* As much as we might like to believe that we're independent as singles, we really are not. We need others.

"Friendship is a sheltering tree."
Samuel Taylor Coleridge[14]

Even when you meet someone special, you will still need other people within your circle. In fact, it is essential to have a community when you meet someone. The people in my community have been able to help me see things about men that I couldn't see in my infatuated state. They have been a safeguard for me multiple times. Members of your community can offer an objective perspective. Your community may help you to avoid a disastrous mistake. When you have your community in your life, listen to them! In healthy relationships, people will have your best interests in mind. A strong community can help you stay faithful to God's commands. They can hold you to your standards, even

---

[14]www.poetryfoundation.org/poems/44000/youth-and-age-56d222ebca145

when you are tempted to give up. The right community will keep you rooted in who you really are and keep you running towards who you want to become.

"For lack of guidance a nation falls, but victory is won through many advisers." (Proverbs 11:14)

A Future Blessing

Marriage will not change the need for a community. Both members of a couple need friends individually, in addition to friends in common with each another. When you have children, you will want them to play with children who sprang from like-minded families. Some friendships will carry into the rest of your life and spill into your children's lives. You never know the struggles that you will encounter within the context of marriage and parenting. Community is such a blessing to lean on in those times of struggle and uncertainty.

I am thankful to know people that I will trust to care for my future children. (Believe me, that's a strong trust!) I know women that I will be able to share my marital and motherhood struggles with. We have been vulnerable in our times of singleness, and I trust that same vulnerability will carry over when we become married women. I look forward to carrying these deep friendships into new seasons.

Community prepares us for marriage. We learn to be better lovers and anticipate the needs of those around us, in their times of joy and brokenness. We learn to let others serve us and to be vulnerable. We learn to endure the faults of others. We learn forgiveness, both forgiving and being forgiven. Importantly, we also learn our strengths and weaknesses as they relate to relationships.

Pray for the gift of community if you don't have this already. It will come to you, sometimes in unexpected ways! Sometimes, the Lord will even lead you to move churches, workplaces, or geographic locations in order to discover this community. Get rooted in a church home. Asking others for recommend-dations is a great way to find a church. The internet is also a way to research churches, see the experiences of others with that church, and to see what is going on there. Primarily, pray to be placed where God wants you—church home, job, geographically, and otherwise.

Remember that a solid community is not built overnight. Be hopeful and prayerful when the seeds of new friendships are planted. Invest time into positive relationships. Sometimes, you will need to sacrifice in order to invest in these relationships, but that investment is well worth it. When you have a loving community in your life, it's truly a gift to be treasured. I'm rooting and praying for you as you grow and deepen your healthy community!

CHAPTER 18

Prayer

A tremendous gift that singles have is the freedom of life that allows for more structured prayer time. I realize that most of you reading have many obligations and commitments. However, overall, singlehood tends to offer more free time and flexibility than marriage and parenthood. It's important to carve out that space with God now. It will benefit your marriage, family, and even future generations. It will get you in the habit of being jealous for your time with God and finding ways to make it happen.

Pray Ahead of Time

Without even knowing them, you can give your spouse one of the greatest gifts: the covering of prayer! In fact, you can even begin now to pray for your future children! What an advantage it is to be able to pray for the future regarding our spouses and children, knowing that prayer is efficacious! *Through our prayers, we can love them before we even meet them.* It is never too early! These prayers that you are praying years ahead of time will be like extra padding and protection. God is not bound by time or space. You don't know exactly what your spouse is going through. You don't know the struggles your future offspring will have in their lives. *But God does, and hears your prayers for them.*

Pray over the individual plan that God has for you and your future spouse. He created both you and your future spouse with a purpose in mind. Pray also for what God has for you as a couple and family. As you become more in tune with the Holy Spirit, you may be given specific prayer points to pray over your spouse or family. Some people even keep journals or notebooks of these prayers for their future spouses. It's so inspiring to hear stories of people praying for their spouses for specific intentions before they even met them, and then to hear the stories of how these prayers were being answered in the time period they were being prayed for! God is truly amazing!

Pray for purity, for yourself and your future spouse. You never know how they are struggling. Chastity is an important topic to intercede about daily because we have no idea whom or what temptations are in their path right now in this area (unless the Holy Spirit tells you, or you already know them and have a good idea that they are the one you'll eventually marry)!

Pray that your future spouse will grow in their relationship with God. Pray for spiritual maturity. This quality has become more important to me as time passes. I want a man who has a history with God. Whatever life has brought him through, I want a man that has clung to God and learned to truly trust Him in every circumstance. I want a man who is convicted about his beliefs in his own heart—not a man who believes because he was raised a certain way or does so out of duty.

Pray against generational curses.[15] All family trees have rotten fruits and diseases (physical, mental, and otherwise) that have been passed down. Every family needs healing. For our children and the generations that follow, we must fight for wholeness! They don't need to suffer the same ways that we or our family members have. You can be the one committed to breaking the pattern. Pray for the family tree of your future spouse also. Talk about what the past and current generations of your families have struggled with. Discuss the strengths of each of your families as well. These are important discussions to have with someone you are considering marrying or becoming engaged to. Keep praying

---

[15] http://www.scborromeo.org/prayers/familytree.pdf

for your current and future family together when you become engaged and married.

"But from everlasting to everlasting the Lord's love is with those who fear Him, and His righteousness with their children's children—with those who keep His covenant and remember to obey His precepts."
(Psalm 103:17-18)

Don't underestimate the power of prayer. More victories are won through prayer than we can ever imagine. Peace is gained through a life of prayer. Your prayer is an armor that will cover you, your future spouse, and your family. Prayer is communication with your Savior. Find what methods of prayer work for you. Importantly, also learn to *listen* to God during your prayer time. Praise is another important aspect of prayer. There is much more to praying than bringing your list of petitions. Spend time praising God and focusing on the great things He has done and will do for you. Praise Him in advance for those things you are praying for!

Stick to your prayer time as if it's the most important thing in your life. Because, truly, it is. All the other aspects of your life will flow from a well-nourished and watered soul.

CHAPTER 19

Faithfulness

Nowadays, commitment is often seen as a dirty word. The culture (at least in America) glorifies doing what you want, when you want, and being unencumbered. Commitment is seen as a mark of weakness. As evidenced in our faith, God shows us that commitment is important! The Father sent His only Son to earth. Jesus then gave Himself up totally and completely for our salvation. There is no greater example of faithfulness than that! The example of Jesus Christ on the cross reveals to us that love equals commitment. Love means pouring yourself out in ways that stretch you to your limits.

Practice Faithfulness Now

Faithfulness is a vital ingredient for a successful marriage. There are ways that we can prepare for that life of faithfulness as singles. This faithfulness manifests in different areas of our lives. Be faithful to God and the purpose He has put in your life now. Living your purpose is the perfect place to be found! Be faithful to keeping God and prayer first. Practice faithfulness and loyalty to those whom God has placed in your life. These practices of faithfulness strengthen you to be faithful in future aspects of your life. Faithfulness is a testimony to God's power to a world which knows more about brokenness and division.

"Let love and faithfulness never leave you;
bind them around your neck,
write them on the tablet of your heart.
Then you will win favor and a good name in the sight of God and man."'
(Proverbs 3:3-4)

I need to be honest about one of the difficulties of being single for an extended period. I've had different days, even seasons, where I simply felt *done* with being single. There were days when I wanted to throw in the towel and trade the "single" chapter of life for "married." Some days, my single reality still seems surreal—it just didn't cross my mind that this journey would be quite so long. I watch people much younger than myself marry and have children. People who I spoke with years ago, without marriage in their life plans, have married. Even then, my heart ached. *It is beyond my human understanding.* In many ways, the journey can become wearisome. It seems like it should be so simple, doesn't it? You meet someone that you're attracted to in various ways. You start "talking." It goes well, and keeps going well. Then, there comes a beautiful day when you become engaged to each other! You meet at the altar, profess your vows, and you're married! When I was younger, I truly believed that it was a simple process. The reality is, this road is a long one. Even when you meet your spouse, the road to the altar may not run entirely smoothly. Sometimes it isn't a linear path. You might not have a great first impression of each other. You might break up a time (or two) before you become engaged. This path of life is surely unexpected. We are given many opportunities to practice faithfulness to God, others, and our true values.

Each day is a test of faith. I don't know when singleness will be over. In fact, the Bible never promises us that we will find a spouse. Our Heavenly Father's promises for us are good, but only He knows what those promises are and what is good for each of us individually.

There are days when finding a man who would be well-suited for me seems impossible. I choose to put my trust in the God who is in the business of doing the impossible! *A delay is not a denial.* Though you may have been praying for years and "working on yourself" (by the grace of God), because you are still waiting now does not mean that it won't happen. I don't fully understand why some of us are called to carry this cross longer than others, but I do know that at any moment, our states can change. Most of all, I know that God is faithful. We, too, are called to be faithful to whatever and wherever He calls us. That means being faithful to *when* He calls us as well. Are you ready for your prayers to be answered? On the other side, are you ready to continue waiting longer than expected?

You are called to be faithful now, to God and all the people He has put in your life to love, even and *especially* when you don't understand His plan. *Faithfulness*—it's a beautiful, painful, and pouring-out word. It pushes you to your very limits. It steers you to rely on God and *His* faithfulness in your life. The choice is yours: be faithful or go your own way. Make the choice to rely on Jesus for the strength that you don't possess within yourself any longer.

Faithfulness hurts. I pour myself out, day by day. I believe that this faithfulness is preparing me for another kind of faithfulness one day: pouring myself out daily in marriage and parenthood. Faithfulness fulfills. I pray that my faithfulness now—to love, to the callings right in front of me, to the Lord—will pay off for my future spouse, our family, and those whom we represent Christ to.

For whatever reason, you are exactly where you are at this moment in time. The people in your vicinity are the ones you are called to love and serve. Whatever task you are about, whether it be ministry, a job, schooling, caring for family members, or even resting and healing while the Lord does His work: that is what you are called to be faithful to until that door shuts. Be a joyful single as you faithfully live out this season. This will help you transition into being a joyful married person one day, if that's a call for you to fulfill.

Deep down, we all desire to be surrounded by faithfulness. We desire friends and family who are faithful to us. When we experience betrayal or disloyalty, it is deeply hurtful. Very importantly, we desire to see God's faithfulness manifest in our lives. As we desire others to reveal their faithfulness to us, we must also be faithful people. Faithfulness begins in the little things. Your "yes" today will pave the way for even greater "yeses" tomorrow and beyond.

CHAPTER 20

Surrender

"**I** want it." This was one of the most common phrases I heard when I worked with a classroom of toddlers. They all wanted the same toy at the exact same time. Yet, in some ways, we are not much different from toddlers. When we want something, *we want it.* Putting off desires is difficult—especially when it's unclear why those desires are currently unattainable. This can be exactly the case with a long season of singleness. It often doesn't make sense, and our desires and the realities of others lead us to believe that marriage should also be our portion. We want marriage, and we want to be married now! For goal-oriented people, it can be especially difficult that this goal is one which hasn't come quite as easily. In moments of difficulty, sometimes singles succumb to the thought that marriage will make suffering more bearable, or even that suffering will decrease during marriage. Strong desires can blind people to the reality.

Clinging to His Vision

Have you ever stubbornly clung to something, even though it was clear you couldn't hold onto it any longer? Maybe, like me, you clung tightly to the dreams of marriage and parenthood occurring by a certain age. Perhaps there is a type of job that you desperately hope for, but your numerous applications seem to be getting no further than the company's trashcan (whether real or electronic). The experience of "clinging" is a human one. We want security and surety. Learning to let go leaves us empty-handed and puts us at the total mercy of God. That is the safest place to be, even when it feels like the most painful and desolate.

For so long, I clung to my vision of life. I believed that I would *definitely* be married with a baby by 28, at the latest. The timeline going any later than that didn't seem like a real possibility. To my dismay, the months and years continued to tick by. Relationships failed, or actually succeeded in their purpose, as I discovered that we were not meant to be together. I tried to run away from the fact that my Creator was leading me on a different path than I ever thought would ever be a part of my life. I tried various ways to meet my husband, including online dating. None of them put me in the path of "the one." From the time I graduated high school, I had the idea that I would go back for a graduate degree in my forties. I pictured my children being out of the house, or almost out of the house, by that time. Looking back, I can't help but laugh. My timeline for my life became turned upside down. Ever heard the adage, "Make God laugh, tell Him your plans"? That saying reminds me of my own life.

In my mid-twenties, it became clear that my job wasn't going to be sustainable. I dearly loved the clients I worked with and the purpose which I found in the work. Yet, I couldn't deny the fact that I was feeling strongly led to obtain a Master's degree so that I could become a Licensed Professional Counselor (LPC). Confirmation and encouragement came from countless sources about following that path. At first, deciding to begin that path was difficult. What made it so difficult, you ask? *Going that way meant that I was abandoning my original plans and blueprint for my life.* It meant that I was surrendering to a completely different direction for my life. It signified that I was surrendering to God's plan, which included a longer period of singleness. His plan was turning out to be *drastically* different than mine. There were rough patches on that path of surrendering to another timeline. It was immensely difficult to be the only one earning an income, while also dealing with the demands of going to school. The life of a single person can be unstable at times. My moves to different living situations are adding up. *Yet, there is abundant grace.* Surrender was difficult, but everything I needed was provided for on my school journey. Even in the difficulties of singleness, my Heavenly Father has poured out tremendous graces to assist me in walking this call out.

I pray that this time is fruitful for my future and that of my future family, as well as the clients I counsel. The time that our Heavenly Father gives us for life is not purposeless or meaningless. I know that my steps are ordered perfectly. I only see the present. **Yet, my Creator sees the whole picture of my life, the life of my future family, and all of history!** I am learning to trust Him more. Each step of trust means abandoning my ideas of how my life should go and surrendering to a different plan or timeline. Surrender is painful. But when you surrender, you are surrendering to Love. This is even when the pain of surrender is crushing. You are surrendering to the One who will be the King of your heart and life, both now and eternally. Our plans for our lives on this earth can't even compare one iota to what God has planned for our eternity. Our plans for our lives can't even compare to the dreams He has for us here! I'm learning more to cling to *His* complete and full vision.

> *"However, as it is written: "What*
> *no eye has seen, what no ear has*
> *heard, and what no human mind has*
> *conceived" -- the things God has*
> *prepared for those who love Him. "*
> *(1 Corinthians 2:9)*

I can't say that surrendering means a fairytale ending on this earth. We were never promised a life without sacrifices and hardships. In fact, Jesus advised us of the opposite. However, our Heavenly Father is always pouring out blessings on us. Even in the most difficult times, His light is always shining into our darkness. He is preparing great things for us.

> *"Let us not become weary in doing*
> *good, for at the proper time we will*
> *reap a harvest if we do not give up. "*
> *(Galatians 6:9)*

Lay It All Down

Keep laying your hopes and dreams before the throne of your Savior. Even if you've been petitioning for decades, don't stop! Be honest with God about what you are feeling and where you are mentally. Yet, be ready to lay it all down once again. Each of us has various things we need to lay in the tomb as we fully surrender to God's plan for our lives. Only you know what your tomb will carry. Allow yourself to grieve your unmet desires, both spoken and unspoken. Grief is a necessary process as we shed our hopes and clothe ourselves in the hopes which God has for our lives. While we lay our dreams into the tomb, it's also important to remember that, as Christians, we are Resurrection people! Christ can resurrect these desires into realities, or bring to life new and beautiful dreams within our lives.

A few examples of what you might lay in your particular tomb:

- The dream of meeting your spouse during a certain year
- The dream of being married by a certain age
- The dream of a relationship happening in a certain way
- The dream of marrying a certain person
- The dream of having a certain person or people attend or be in your wedding
- The dream of being a "young" parent and an empty nester by a certain age
- The dream of having biological children or a certain number of children

- The dream of following a certain career path
- The dream of your career being "successful" by a certain age

Grief has many layers. It's a complicated thing that can rear its head in the most unexpected and interesting ways. You may not even consciously realize what exactly it is that you are grieving. Be patient with yourself, and don't be afraid of letting yourself feel the pain. Walking into a reality which you never planned for, and even dreaded, is a sorrowful experience. Yet, in the midst of grief, remember God's power. You surrender and lay your dreams in the tomb, your heart crushed by the sacrifice. Yet Christ may choose to resurrect what you have placed in the tomb in miraculous, unexpected, and surprising ways. It's up to us to surrender all to Him and let Him be God!

As paradoxical as it sounds, there is freedom in letting go. There is relief in giving over our tightly-held plans to the One with a master plan. Friends, we are simply not in control of our lives! Thank God, too, because how difficult a thing is would be to truly be in control. However, making the decision to surrender to God is one of the most difficult decisions we can make. What have you surrendered to God? What areas still need to be surrendered completely to Him?

The Cross and Us

I once heard an analogy about a person who wanted to choose another cross. They believed the cross they had was not fit for them. It seemed too heavy and too much to bear. Jesus allowed them to choose another cross. He led them into a room filled with crosses of various sizes hanging on the wall. The person was drawn to a small cross that looked easy to bear compared to the other crosses, which looked heavy and unbearable. They pointed out this small cross to Jesus. "The cross you've chosen is the cross that you are already carrying," Jesus told them.

This story can relate immensely to our journey as singles. The cross seems unbearable sometimes. To singles, marriage often appears much easier than being alone. Yet, you probably don't know what's on the other side of the immaculate Instagram or Facebook posts of married couples. You don't know what they *aren't* saying when they gush about their spouse and married life. You don't know the struggles they cry themselves to sleep over, or fight over daily with their spouse. You don't know that they actually regret their decision of marrying that person, or deal daily with some form of abuse. What is seen on the surface is often much different than the reality. Many singles romanticize marriage and forget that it, too, will have its crosses.

I know how desperately you long to throw off the heavy cross that weighs on you, and to be freed of it. **Yet, the cross is what connects us to Christ.** It doesn't matter what the specific cross is. As you endure suffering, you can more clearly feel the love that Jesus had for you as He gave everything, enduring any type of suffering imaginable. Suffering even allows one to empathize with others who are carrying their crosses, and to help them bear their burdens. You would not be holding this book in your hands if it were not for my experience carrying this cross of extended singleness.

Throughout this journey, I've had to let go of control. This is a decision that I've had to make over and over as new situations arise. As I've learned to listen to God and trust Him, I've repeatedly seen His faithfulness. I pray that, as you begin or continue the journey of surrender, you are encouraged at the Heavenly Father's love for you. Instead of anger and feeling that God is withholding from you, I pray that you know He has the fullness of time and your life in His hands. I pray that you open your hands to receive the gifts that are present in this season of your life—even if they are gifts that you never specifically prayed for—and especially if they are gifts that you never desired.

"If you, then, though you are evil,
know how to give good gifts to your
children, how much more will your
Father in Heaven give good gifts to
those who ask Him!"
(Matthew 7:11)

Earlier in my journey of being single longer than expected, I didn't experience the healing power of hope. Unfortunately, most of my hope revolved around the hope of getting married—and soon. The state of marriage is its own gift. Yet, remember how St. Paul talked about singleness. *It, too, is a gift.* There are gifts within gifts. For some, we may find these gifts in singleness: learning patience, and trusting the Lord. Other gifts we could experience in singleness are time to focus on other ventures and (God willing) build solid foundations for a future family. For each of us individually, there are other specific gifts to be found in singleness.

The cross of (possibly temporary) singleness may be keeping you from the heavier cross of a dreadful marriage. Much of the cross of singleness is the *waiting*. It seems like endless waiting sometimes. We live on planet Earth. As long as we're here, we will always have crosses to carry. However, I believe that waiting on the suitable partner that God has for you will keep you from bearing unnecessary crosses that were never yours to carry. Friend, you can't run any longer. It is time to surrender to what God has for your life. It's time to allow your Heavenly Father to pry your plan of life from your hands and allow the Holy Spirit to blow in with His marvelous plan for you. As long as you continue to cling, you will never know exactly what He has in mind.

CHAPTER 21

Faith and Hope for the Future

The Father promises us in Jeremiah 29:11: "For I know the plans I have for you," declares the Lord, "plans to prosper you and not to harm you, plans to give you hope and a future." If we kept this at the forefront of our minds each day, I wonder how different our way of living would be? I believe that we would be more joyful people, secure in the knowledge that *God's got us*!

Our Heavenly Father created us with great things in mind for our lives. For many singles, often unintentionally, marriage becomes the overarching goal. Marriage becomes the "hope" for the future. Parenthood becomes one of the strongest desires of the heart. Some lose track of other hopes for their lives, believing in marriage as the ultimate hope. This is dangerous for a few reasons.

Earthly Marriage: Not Our Ultimate Hope

We are to serve no God but God. In Exodus 20:3, we are told to have no other gods besides Him. Each time we place anything above God in our lives, that is idolatry. When we seek our own will above all, we are closing ourselves off to God's will. We are placing something else above God and His intents and purposes. This is not the same type of idolatry as worshipping a golden calf. Nevertheless, it is still idolatry. Be honest with God about what you have come to idolize in your life, and be determined to center yourself back on Him.

If marriage is the ultimate goal, both singleness and marriage become disappointing. If you don't end up getting married, or wait years longer for marriage, you may become bitter at this unrealized goal. When marriage becomes a goal sought to the detriment of other things, one forgets that knowing God's will and loving Him should be the ultimate aim. What happens when getting married is the highest hope, and that marriage becomes a reality? That marriage, and that partner, will bring disappointment. No person or marriage can live up to the burden of all hope being placed on them. Only Jesus can live up to that. Because marriage was the central goal, there will come a moment of awakening: there is more. The person's heart will still be unsettled due to making marriage the goal and losing sight of other aspects. If marriage is the goal, then what's next after a person is married? Our hearts are restless until they find complete rest in their Creator. Deeper joy in the gifts that each season of life offer spring from that contentment in the Creator.

The Need for Hope

Living in hope brings freedom. *When we lose hope, we live in anxiety and fear.* We lose our joy and our center. Hope lifts the shackles of worry off us. It protects and preserves. When we lose hope, we lose faith in the thing we hoped for! ***If we are no longer hoping, we might miss it when what we hoped for comes along!*** We serve a good, good Father. His plans are not always our plans. His timing, especially, often does not line up with human expectations. There is no problem in hoping for marriage. The problem comes when marriage becomes the ultimate goal. We must place our ultimate hope in Jesus Christ.

Hoping brings a sense of peace and cheerfulness to our lives. Being bitter and living without hope does not add any positivity to your life. It certainly isn't attractive to "potentials," either. Don't miss meeting your special person because you are living dejectedly, missing the spirit of hopefulness! It can be difficult to hope or remember what it is like to look forward to something when it hasn't come to pass, or when things seem hopeless in the natural. If you haven't seen the caliber of man or woman that you've been looking for, it's hard to believe that they exist. If you haven't been interviewed for your dream job yet, it can make you wonder if the interview will ever come, let alone the job offer! Hope allows us to view life with a supernatural lens and realize that the present reality can shift immensely.

As Christians, we know that there is good news! **Our faith is the reason for hope!** Faith provides hope not only for this life but also for an everlasting joy! Nothing can compare to that! Faith allows us to walk with supernatural vision and expectations, not relying on what our limited human vision can see. Faith is the sustenance that enables us to walk through a desert filled with trials, knowing that we'll find refreshing water up ahead—even when all we can see is our dehydration, the hot sand, snakes, and what seems like endless miles to go.

'Therefore, the promise comes by faith, so that it may be by grace and may be guaranteed to all Abraham's offspring—not only to those who are of the law but also to those who have the faith of Abraham. He is the father of us all. As it is written: "I have made you a father of many

nations." He is our father in the sight of God, in whom he believed—the God who gives life to the dead and calls into being things that were not. Against all hope, Abraham in hope believed and so became the father of many nations, just as it had been said to him, "So shall your offspring be." Without weakening in his faith, he faced the fact that his body was as good as dead—since he was about a hundred years old—and that Sarah's womb was also dead. Yet he did not waver through unbelief regarding the promise of God, but was strengthened in his faith and gave glory to God, being fully persuaded that God had power to do what he had promised. This is why "it was credited to him as righteousness." The words "it was credited to him" were written not for him alone, but also for us, to whom God will credit righteousness—for us who believe in Him who raised Jesus our Lord from the dead."
(Romans 4:16-24)

When you learn to trust in God's goodness and loving plan for our life, it will keep you from losing hope. You'll walk confidently in purpose. As Christians, we are Resurrection people. We have many things to hope for, friends! Only one of them is marriage. More than anything else, we hope for Heaven, where worry will be no more. Grief will be no more. *Waiting* will be no more.

When you place your hope in the Lord, He will keep you centered. As you continue to seek Him, He will keep your hope secure and in the right places. Guard yourself against desperation in regard to finding a spouse. It is not godly or attractive. It scares people away. If desperation does attract anyone, it will almost certainly be another desperate person. *Do not settle.* Believe me when I say I know the temptation. I know the lonely nights. I know the feeling of thinking that you should have gone past this stage of life a long time ago. I know that sometimes, it can feel like you're living an alternate reality. It's a mystery that's difficult to understand to our human eyes. I know that sometimes, feelings of desperation can creep in. Bring these feelings to God. Reflect on what is causing the desperation. ***Remember this: it is far more preferable to be single than to be with someone who you are not meant to be with.*** Temporary happiness is nothing compared to a lifetime of joy. Temporary happiness can quickly turn to a lifetime of misery. This is not the plan that God has for our marriages.

I want to shout it so all the world can hear: *the plans that God has for each of us are good!* The plans may not be what you expect. Usually, they aren't what we expect, or they do not happen in the manner we expect. Perhaps those plans will involve a loving husband and family. If you're a man, maybe the plan will include a lovely wife and children. Sometimes, there is another plan for your life. We must accept whatever He wills. No matter the plan or realities of our lives—He is full of love toward us, an overflowing love. I'm learning to rest in His loving arms. I try not to fight, but so much I still do. There are days I want *my own plan,* instead of His— because at the moment, His plan does not always make sense! Perhaps you can relate.

If there is one thing I've learned, it's that *singleness is a daily lesson in trust.* We have no idea what tomorrow will bring. We have no idea if we will have a special person by our side the next year, in five years, or even within a decade. The not knowing, the longing, is meant to lead us to trust. Without trust, we would go crazy. Learning to trust teaches us contentment. It shows us that we are not in control. Contentment allows us to be at peace, no matter what our circumstances may be.

One thing that I've reflected on a lot is the drastic differences in God's plans for different people. Why do some people find their spouses early on, while others wait decades? I don't have all the answers; I still have many questions of my own. Yet, I do know that Our Heavenly Father wants us to keep continually looking to Him. He wants us to trust and rely on Him fully. He accomplishes His purposes in different ways than humans normally expect. In fact, His plan and ways are so often the exact opposite of what we would have chosen! We need to keep looking to Him for the next move and to learn to recognize when His work looks different than we expected. We must learn to recognize the gifts which are being offered to us within the distinct seasons and different stories of our lives.

"For My thoughts are not your thoughts, neither are your ways My ways," declares the LORD. 'As the heavens are higher than the earth, so are My ways higher than your ways and My thoughts than your thoughts.'"
(Isaiah 55:8-9)

In every aspect of your life, your Creator has plans of love! Those plans of love consist of more than marriage. Seek the blessings in each season and area of your life. Stand on the promise of God being God, not in the promise of marriage. Hope for marriage, if that's the desire of your heart and God hasn't steered you otherwise. Just remember that life is more than marriage and don't make it your ultimate goal.

Be vigilant. Above all, keep your heart focused on Him. When you focus on the Lover of your soul, you can't go wrong. God is a good Father, and He does not forsake His children.

I am so eager for you to see the good plans that He has for you come to fruition in your life! Keep hoping and keep praying. Rejoice in the greatness up ahead for you, here and eternally! Your "different story" is a story that the world needs to hear. Keep on walking.

Dear Heavenly Father,

I thank you for each individual reading this book! Thank You for their different stories and that no one else can make the exact mark on this world that they can. Thank You for how they will continue to shape the world and make it a better place. Thank You even for their trials which they thought would break them but through which You will actually bring about the greatest victories of their lives! Continue to heal their hearts and bring wholeness into each facet of their lives. Thank You for all the great things that You have planned for them, and especially that You plan to provide them an unimaginably joyful eternity! Strengthen them for the journey up ahead. Let no weapon formed against them prosper. Surround them with positive people who are seeking Your will and to love You. Allow them to recognize the numerous gifts and graces present within their lives now. Give them the vision to recognize their identity in You, and to daily rest in the love which sent Jesus to the cross to sacrifice His very self for them. Give them peace and joy as they hope for marriage. Give them the grace of clarity when you bring the person into their life whom You are inviting them to give their unhindered "yes" to. Thank You, Heavenly Father, for all these things. I pray them all in the precious and holy name of Jesus.

Amen!

Epilogue

B y the grace of God, I've come to a peaceful place in my journey of singleness. I am 31 years old as I (finally!) finish writing this book. My Heavenly Father continues to confirm that He does have marriage in the plans for me. I just don't know when or who. I'm rejoicing in the great gifts that He has placed in my life now, while expectantly awaiting the gifts that are to come.

I have faith that, one day, the struggles of my life will change. Singleness will be a cross of long ago, and instead, I'll bear the joyous responsibility of loving and serving my husband and our children. My sisters (who were also once single) and I will call each other up from wherever our respective families have made our abode. We'll be holding babies on our hips, our toddlers constantly calling us by our new title of "mom," making it difficult to have one of the long conversations we've grown accustomed to. Our fingers will carry the rings that symbolize the covenant we've prayed so long for. The most important (earthly) relationships we have will be with the men we yearned for, prayed for, and fasted for without even knowing their name. We'll be weary from pouring out our love every day in different ways than we do now.

Friends, I'm eager to write the next story: the story that God is writing as I write this book! I look forward to writing the story of my husband and me, and the creative way that God brings us together. I can honestly say now that I am grateful for my long journey of singleness. There have been abundant gifts and treasures along this long road. God had to allow me to go through a deep healing and transformation so that I could be most effective in all that He is calling me to do. Most of all, I had to grow closer to His heart and learn to desire Him above all.

Each day, I'm living a different story than I ever expected I would be. Woven into this story are beauty, joy, and triumph amidst all the struggles. With me is the Author of it all, making it all beautiful in its time. Without my "different story," I wouldn't be writing to you. I wouldn't have a heart that strongly empathizes with other singles—something difficult to do for those who haven't had the experience of being single for a long time.

I don't know exactly where your different story will lead. I do know that it can lead you to the expansive heart of the Father, Who has always been waiting with outstretched arms for you. Following Him will draw you deeper into the story that was written for you before time even began, when the

Creator of all decided that the world would be a better place with you in it.

Thank you for coming along on this journey. I know it's not a journey that you packed for, and it has been very weary. I pray that reading this book has given you some nourishment for the path. Even if you don't feel like you will make it, I know you can! Rejoice and take heart, friend, as you continue to step forward on this beautiful, crazy "different story," which our Creator laid out for you. You are not alone. You have been chosen and redeemed. You are loved, now and forever. Your life is a work in progress, but the Author of it all is making it into a masterpiece.

> *"He has made everything beautiful in its time. He has also set eternity in the human heart; yet no one can fathom what God has done from beginning to end."*
> *(Ecclesiastes 3:11)*

Recommended Reading

25 Ways to Prepare for Marriage Other Than Dating by Jamal Miller

Boundaries in Dating: Making Dating Work by Henry Cloud and John Townsend

Captivating by John Eldredge and Stasi Eldredge

For Men Only: A Straightforward Guide to the Inner Lives of Women by Shaunti Feldhahn

For Women Only: What You Need to Know about the Inner Lives of Men by Shaunti Feldhahn

Glorious Meeting: How to Receive One's Spouse from the Heart of God? by Denis and Suzel Bourgerie

How to Avoid Falling In Love With a Jerk by John Van Epp

How to Find Your Soulmate Without Losing Your Soul by Jason and Crystalina Evert

How to Overcome Heartbreak: Recovering from Misguided Love by Nicole D. Miller, MBA

How to Overcome Heartbreak: Stories that Heal by Nicole D. Miller, MBA

One Beautiful Dream by Jennifer Fulwiler

Red Flags: How to Know When You're Dating a Loser by Gary S. Aumiller and Daniel Goldfarb

Switch on Your Brain: The Key to Peak Happiness, Thinking, and Health by Dr. Caroline Leaf

The 5 Love Languages: The Secret to Love that Lasts by Gary Chapman

The 5 Love Languages Singles Edition: The Secret that Will Revolutionize Your Relationships by Gary Chapman

The Prayer That Heals: Praying for Healing in the Family by Francis Macnutt

Things I Wish I'd Known Before We Got Married by Gary Chapman

Three to Get Married by Fulton J. Sheen

My Different
Story/Reflections

MY DIFFERENT STORY/REFLECTIONS

A DIFFERENT STORY

MY DIFFERENT STORY/REFLECTIONS

A DIFFERENT STORY

MY DIFFERENT STORY/REFLECTIONS

A DIFFERENT STORY

A DIFFERENT STORY

_____

_____

_____

_____

_____

_____

_____

_____

_____

_____

_____

_____

_____

_____

_____

_____

A DIFFERENT STORY

Keep trusting the
Greatest Author.
Your story has only begun!

Made in the USA
Monee, IL
03 March 2021